A GARLAND TO SYLVIA

THE MACMILLAN COMPANY
NEW YORK · BOSTON · CHICAGO
ATLANTA · SAN FRANCISCO

MACMILLAN & CO., Limited
LONDON · BOMBAY · CALCUTTA
MELBOURNE

THE MACMILLAN CO. OF CANADA, Ltd.
TORONTO

A GARLAND TO SYLVIA

A Dramatic Reverie

WITH A PROLOGUE

BY
PERCY MACKAYE

WILDSIDE PRESS

COPYRIGHT, 1910,
By THE MACMILLAN COMPANY.

Set up and electrotyped. Published May, 1910.

This play has been copyrighted and published simultaneously in the United States and Great Britain. All acting rights, both professional and amateur, are reserved in the United States, Great Britain, and countries of the Copyright Union, by Percy MacKaye. Performances forbidden and right of representation reserved. Application for the right of performing this piece must be made to The Macmillan Company. Any piracy or infringement will be prosecuted in accordance with the penalties provided by the United States Statutes: —

"Sec. 4966. — Any person publicly performing or representing any dramatic or musical composition, for which copyright has been obtained, without the consent of the proprietor of the said dramatic or musical composition, or his heirs or assigns, shall be liable for damages therefor, such damages in all cases to be assessed at such sum, not less than one hundred dollars for the first and fifty dollars for every subsequent performance, as to the Court shall appear to be just. If the unlawful performance and representation be wilful and for profit, such person or persons shall be guilty of a misdemeanor, and upon conviction be imprisoned for a period not exceeding one year." U. S. Revised Statutes, Title 60, Chap. 3.

Persons desiring to read in public this play, or any other play by the author, are requested first to confer with the author through the publishers.

Norwood Press
J. S. Cushing Co. — Berwick & Smith Co.
Norwood, Mass., U.S.A.

To
ARVIA
AND HER MOTHER

PREFACE

THIS play was begun in the autumn of 1896, when its author was a senior in Harvard College. After graduation in 1897, work upon it was postponed for more than a year, but was resumed during the autumn and winter of 1898 and 1899, in Italy, where the larger part was written and the whole completed at the Villa Aldobrandini, Frascati, near Rome. After a year spent in completing other dramatic work in Germany, the tentative dramatist, returning in 1900 to America, secured through "Sylvia" his first professional commission — from E. H. Sothern for "The Canterbury Pilgrims" — and his first professional criticism: two columns by Norman Hapgood in *The New York Commercial Advertiser*.

So much account of this play is pertinent to place it rightly among those which the writer has already put forth, and to preface a few reasons for its publication at this time.

Fourteen years ago, in America, the vocation of dramatist held a backward and unenviable status compared with to-day. To-day, to be sure, it is still sufficiently retrograde, still vastly capable of cultivation, yet at least it has begun to wield a power which is itself awakening public opinion and artistic impulse in behalf of its nobler growth. To glance back into the last century is to be reassured of this.

In 1896, leadership in the drama as a native expression or technical craft could hardly be said to have commenced in our country. A young American, planning to adopt the profession of playwriting strictly as an art, must have sought far and probably in vain through theatre, press, university, society in general, for any adequate modern standards critical or creative. To search abroad would avail him little more. Most of the European and English dramatists and critics, who have done so much to leaven the world-thought of the last decade — names such as Hauptmann, Sudermann, Maeterlinck, D'Annunzio, Rostand, Hervieu, Brandes, Archer, Shaw, Phillips, Barrie — would probably be strange in his ears. Even Ibsen, then chiefly notorious for his "Doll's House," was still a vague rumor, caricatured or belittled. As a result, our apprentice would probably turn — both for technique and creative instigation — to the only perennial master of English dramatic tradition. He would turn to Shakspere, printed or acted, and, whirled into the surging vortex of that inspiration, he would be fortunate if he escaped the misleading attractions of his archaic craftsmanship and Titanic mannerism. He would be doubly fortunate if, by the effort of that mighty emulation, he were not deflected from expressing his own soul.

PREFACE

As the record of an apprentice in American drama, striving sincerely to express himself under conditions of that period, this play may perhaps have its interest for the historical critic.

As an expression peculiarly of youth, and the vision of youth, it may also make its appeal to the philosopher of immaturity.

Immaturity, being as old as man, needs no man's apology. Yet youth is himself in such haste and hot desire to mature that he has no time to defend his intrenchments against the condescending sallies of maturity. Viewed by his elders as merely a passing phase of human nature, youth rebels, and is ever in the act of claiming permanent human representation when, of his own accord, he yields allegiance to the complacent majority of the mature. Like a radical in the commons, raised unexpectedly to the peerage, youth is satisfied by the recognition of sovereign time and becomes conservative. "Promising young man!" exclaims the sage, and the world murmurs approvingly. "Promising old fellow?" queries the boy, but gets no "rise" out of the world.

To be one and twenty is a dubious prerogative granted but once to one and all of us: but not to one at a time. Fortunately the privilege is conferred in phalanxes, so that the immature prophet may always speak his message to a moving phalanx of his peers.

It is perhaps chiefly as the technical confession of a dramatic apprentice for the imaginations of dramatic apprentices that this conception of one-and-twenty may be of some service to-day. For "Sylvia" is not merely a youthful Dramatic Reverie; it is a young dramatist's reverie; and in America, to-day is peculiarly the day of young dramatists, though their reveries are happily not of as isolated a character as that of Felix in "The Prologue." Indeed, if the date of "The Prologue" were 1910 instead of 1896, it is safe to say that Felix's initiation would consist in reading his play aloud to an eager and merciless audience of seniors, whose pockets would be bulging with their own dramatic efforts.

To-day a new growth of fellowship has sprung up among the younger play-makers and play-critics, and especially in the universities this growth has become an authentic university movement, under the critical leadership, at Harvard, of Professor George Pierce Baker. To him peculiarly the universities and the nation owe a permanent debt of gratitude for his patient and enlightened championship of an ideal, long ignored, pregnant with vital importance to our civilization — the ideal of cultivating, at the fountain heads of the liberal arts, living standards of excellence in the living drama. In this respect, the Harvard Dramatic Club holds an unique position among college dramatic associations, by intelligently devoting its energies not to amateur show-making or archaic revivals, but to technical stagecraft in the acting and writing of modern plays.

PREFACE xiii

Results of this Harvard work on the professional stage are already beginning to be seen, and the acted plays of Edward Sheldon and Hermann Hagedorn promise a larger fulfilment. The most signal expression of it, manifesting the vital significance of a present day university movement in the acted drama, was the performance at Sanders Theatre, Cambridge, on January 24th this year, of William Vaughn Moody's play "The Faith Healer" by Mr. Henry Miller and his company. On that occasion, for the first time, the dramatic work of a graduate was performed professionally at a great university, and in that fusion of the ideals for which Mr. Moody, as a modern dramatist, Mr. Miller, as an artist of the theatre, and Professor Baker, as a creative critic in the university, have zealously stood, a precedent of national importance was established.

The space of a preface does not permit me to describe specifically important progress in other universities.

The influence, however, of this contemporaneous ideal of the drama is happily not limited to Harvard, but is extending, with accelerating vigor, through American universities, colleges and schools, where it is being demonstrated by scores of progressive men and women. Needless to say, the renascent impulse is also active in dramatic and theatrical work having no connection with the universities and schools; yet nowhere else is it so fraught with the promise of continuity, organization and idealism, correlated with the forces of national leadership.

In the universities to-day, then, the dramatic apprentice finds himself definitely related to the beginnings of a renascence in his art, in a way impossible to the author of "Sylvia." I refer to him in the third person because, for me, the author of this play is a personality strangely commingled of the first and third persons, with emphasis upon the third. "P. W. M." (having not yet dropped the 'Wallace' of his name), a student at Harvard, new to his senior gown; again, a first-year graduate, sharp-edged to the struggling loneliness of life; again a dreamer in Italy, steeped in the old mystic charm of cypressed ruins, the bells of Rome, the hues of Raphael, the moon through falling almond-bloom — that P. W. M., I once knew him well, his joys, his pangs, his doubts, his aspirations. Afterwards I was his critic, his counsellor, his close friend, yet it can hardly be said with truth that we knew each other, for to him I never was; and much that was all in all to him — what was it? — I have forgotten.

It is, therefore, with a certain diffidence that I undertake now to edit and preface his play. In doing so, to put it forth as a work of myself, or as of another, is equally disconcerting; personal apology, disinterested approval, are alike incongruous. Differing as I do in some respects from P. W. M. in his dramatic confession of faith, agreeing as I do in other respects, how can I assume that he would approve me as his prefacer? Happily, from this semi-posthumous dilemma, I have found a living escape: I have found a Preface, written eleven years ago by P. W. M. himself, at a moment when there appeared to be some danger of the play's publication — a danger deferred to the present hour.

That contemporary preface, written in 1899, soon after the play's completion, speaks of "Sylvia" with more insight and authority than I can now, and having been left by P. W. M. together with his play manuscript in my hands, I have felt responsible to print it here without alteration, as follows: —

A FOREWORD
TO
"A GARLAND TO SYLVIA"
by
Percy Wallace MacKaye

I remember once sitting in a crowded theatre and being thrilled by the thought that the thousand eyes around me, riveted on the stage, were unconsciously gazing into the innermost recesses of a poet's mind — filling their myriad-soul with the vision of his single imagination.

This thought has doubtless moved many others besides myself, though it may not have led them to consider many of the possible inferences to be drawn from its truth. Some of these inferences, as relating to the play which follows, I should like to consider here.

First, though, it is but natural that the average spectator of a play should not thus view the stage before him as an objectification of the dramatist's mind; for it is the dramatist's first business to annul himself in his play; to draw attention, that is, to his vision, not to his own personality. And yet, in spite of this, his obvious function of impersonality, the poetic dramatist must always be an unconscious lyrist. "Unconscious," I say, because, though he does not in his work give direct expression to his personal attributes, opinions and longings as the lyric singer does, yet he is impelled by the same motive as all true singers to give expression to his deepest self. For the primal motive of art is the motive of expression — the longing to speak, whether in air, or stone, or tint, or form. The master impulse of every artist, therefore, is to express himself, and a dramatist is essentially an artist.

His means of expression, however, are far more complicated and indirect than those of the simple lyrist. The lyrist sings himself in the expression of his own thoughts, his own emotions, his own character. The dramatist sings himself in the expression of the thoughts of others, the emotions of others, the characters of others; yet of others, whom he has first made a portion of himself in imagination.

Now it is in this imaginative appropriation of his various play-characters — or we may say as truly, *their* appropriation of his expanded being — it is in this inward impersonation of the *dramatis personæ* by the dramatist, or of the dramatist by the *dramatis personæ*, as well as in the first basic motive of artistic expression, that every true dramatist exhibits in his work those essential evidences of uttered personality which mark him as, in truth, a lyrist.

Shakspere is not an exception. He is indeed the most perfect of poets in that he is the most impersonal (so called) of dramatists, wherein that term "impersonal" means no more nor less than this: that his personality has expanded in imagination nearer to the universal than any other. And this kind of personality, as opposed to the individuality whose attributes are merely ephemeral, is that which every true artist seeks by his sympathy, or imagination, to develop, and that which is developed, to its broadest capacity, by the means of expression of the dramatist. These means of expression, as I have mentioned, are the characters, emotions, thoughts of others, imaginized (if I may use the word — meaning thereby both perceived and embodied, discovered and clothed, by his poetic imagination): in other words, human nature itself, which followed to its deepest means Nature herself and mystery.

Now if a young dramatist, with his limited but ever expanding personality, seeks to express himself through characters and traits of human nature, in other words, if he is seeking to write a play, how shall he be most true to that human nature? By studying it through that faculty in him which is most keenly and intellectually observant of the myriad realistic tricks and traits of human character, as mannerisms, "dress," differentiation of speech, etc., which make toward the outward individualizing of men? Or through that faculty, which — passively excluding the moral and intellectual — observes mainly what is æsthetic: the grace, that is, of form, tone, color in life, which

xviii   PREFACE

constitute the groupings and the lights and shades *in se* of human nature? Or through that deepest inclusive beauty in his own nature, which is inseparable alike from what is ethical, æsthetic and intellectual — which is indeed the eye of perfect sympathy — the poetic imagination, love itself?

Struggling deeply in his own heart to solve this choice in truth, a young artist, whose faith-inspired ignorance is at once creating and discovering the ideal which is to lead him to what perhaps is the true solution — we first meet Felix.

When I first conceived this play, it came to me as a veritable vision, if so humble a work may claim that classification. To show the personal, or lyrical, aspect of the play then — and it hung in my fancy then practically as it stands here in print, save for the greater distinctness of actually worded speeches now, which then were the action or emotion they represent — I transcribe this sonnet, which I wrote soon afterward:

Far in a dawn, hid in the dusk of sleep,
   I woke, with silent Somnus at my side;
   We lay in a dim wood, where I descried
A troop of ghostly lovers, such as keep
Upon the stage a parlance strange and deep.
   I spoke to them: they heard not, nor replied.
" Ye phantoms of mine out-thought selves," I cried,
" Are ye not perished? Seek ye still to reap
The love of Sylvia, holy, fair and wise?
   Depart! and be no more." And then methought
I touched their garments, looked them in the eyes,
   Beseeching them; but they beheld me not;
For I was ghost, and they — realities,
   Born of the dark inevitableness of thought.

In this sonnet I would seem to refer to myself as Felix. And indeed I am, or rather was, when I wrote the play; but yet no more Felix than Sylvia, or Babblebrook, or Sandrac, save in as much as one of those may be more deeply true to human nature than another.

Thus, as I began to write the play, this somewhat introspective — though I think not morbid — contemplation of my own relation to my characters fascinated, nay I confess, weighed upon me, with some touch of Felix's doubt and Sandrac's bitterness; so that I was soon struck with the unusual chance to vivify to an audience's imagination the thought with which I began this preface, coupled with another of deeper significance.

I wished to portray — or rather, I saw portrayed before me mentally — first, a young *dramatist*, groping in the mists of his imagination, confronted and confounded by that personality of his own which he had unwittingly but inevitably wrought into the characters of his play; the moral effect — in deeper thought, bitterness, remorse and faith — of the conflict with that inevitability; and thereby the reflex effect of all this upon the audience of my own play, through a clear revelation of the truth that the real stage of the drama is the mind of man.

And secondly, I beheld, and tried to portray, a young *man*, groping in the mystery of our life, where "the living are our ghosts," where both fancy and reality mock us, but where the implanted love of ideality within us leads us to put the awed question to the spirit of mystery, though we know it shall not answer: the question whether "truth itself be but the faith of an aspiring reason," and lastly where to the rational and faithful lover, the beauty of Nature — the daughter of Pan — becomes wedded to his very soul through faith.

This daughter of Pan is Sylvia, though the reader may well rub his eyes twice to discover her classic father in the crotchety Hikrion. It is not my intention here to say much about Hikrion: only this — that I conceived him as still exhibiting, in spite of all Felix's conscious efforts (when he wrote H's part in his own play) to disguise him under a totally different type of character, — as exhibiting the elusive, unsuppressible, spirit of primitive Nature, which underlies all human nature, defying all conscious analysis and characterization. I say this to assist, not to excuse, my impotence to carry out this conception adequately.

One word as to the form: Felix's play (which, as he says, was in a state of incompletion at the time of his initiation at college) is, for clearness' sake, entirely written in *terza rima*,[1] corresponding, in sequence of end-rhyme merely, with Dante's verse in "The Divine Comedy," with the exception of Act II, Scene 2, which is written in Shaksperian sonnets. The verse itself is frequently rough and "run-over" in its phrasings, to conceal the effect of rhyme, since that is used simply to distinguish the more clearly Felix's own play from the main body of the "Reverie," which includes it. Its effect otherwise is bad, as it leads to diffuseness.

And now for this "Garland" of mingled meaning and mysticism, with which the poor reader is supposed to bind his pained brows, the discriminating critic has already found a courteous word of damnation; and indeed I am not far disinclined to join him heartily in the damning. The word is "Allegory," and in that gory alley of Oblivion lies many a sproutling mur-

---

[1] The exact *terza rima* form has been modified in places throughout the play, by revisions and excisions made shortly after the play's completion.

dered in his first blush. But yet, one word for this one, ere the red ink of righteousness leave its deadly scratch on gentle Sylvia.

In birth, at least, "Sylvia" is not of the family Allegory, whatever suspicion and peril her garb and training may now lead her into. I mean that ever in conception throughout the play, the image, or vision, has come first; then after and out of the image — the meaning. Never was it *vice versa*, which I understand to be the true *genus allegoricum*. And Sylvia herself, to me as to Felix, was never a starry nebula of theoretics, but as near and blushing a personality as the ideal which every youth out of a hundred worships in his heart of hearts. Having said so much, dear Sylvia, it is not for me to comment on thy imperfect realization in this play. For thou art Felix's now, and not mine, and he alone can shield thee henceforth.

P. W. M.

FRASCATI, ROME,
 March, 1899.

Such, then, is the Preface of P. W. M., apprentice. As the words of one with whom P. M. — still apprentice, however much he would modify to-day that early confession of faith — has a life-work in common, the writer begs leave to submit them to the proverbial gentleness of the reader.

PERCY MACKAYE.

CORNISH, NEW HAMPSHIRE,
 March, 1910.

CHARACTERS

OF THE PROLOGUE

FELIX CLOUDSLEY, *a Senior in Harvard College.*
HUGH MERRIMAN, } *his classmates.*
WARTON,
OTHER SENIORS.
MR. BERRY, *an old friend of Felix.*
MR. ROURKE, *a retired actor.*
A PROCTOR.
SYLVIA.

OF THE REVERIE

FELIX,
SOMNUS, } *Persons in the World of Reverie.*
THE MIST-MOTHERS,
SYLVIA,

SANDRAC, **an Oxford Student,**
BABBLEBROOK, **a courtier,**
SOB, **a curate,** } *Sylvia's Suitors*
PIERRE, **a painter,**
ALBERTO, **a violinist,**

SYLVIA,
HIKRION, her foster-father, } *Persons in Felix's Play*
FERVIAN,
FLURRIEL, } *her handmaids.*
FRESCA,
SIX OTHERS of her handmaids, } *Non-speaking*
SPIRITS OF FANCY,

ACT I

SCENE FIRST: (The Prologue) — *A room in Hollis Hall, Harvard College. Time, the Present.*

SCENE SECOND:[1] (*Act I of* The Reverie) — *The Forest of Arden, Shakspere's Time. Dawn; afterwards day.*

ACT II

SCENE FIRST: *A Room in Sylvia's Cottage. Day.*

SCENE SECOND: *Sylvia's Garden, surrounded by the Forest. Twilight. Afterwards transformed to Sylvia's Palace; Moonlight.*

ACT III

SCENE: *The Same. Noon.*

ACT IV

SCENE FIRST: *A Cleft in a Mountain.*

SCENE SECOND: *The Forest. Twilight.*

---

[1] The curtain does not fall between Scene First and Scene Second. With Scene Second commences Act I of Felix's Play, of which the action takes place between the dawn of one day and twilight of the next.

A GARLAND TO SYLVIA

Who is Sylvia? What is she,
  That all her swains commend her?
Holy, fair and wise is she:
  The heaven such grace did lend her
That admirèd she might be.

Is she kind as she is fair?
  For beauty lives with kindness.
To her eyes love doth repair
  To help him of his blindness,
And, being helped, inhabits there.

Then to Sylvia let us sing
  That Sylvia is excelling.
She excels each mortal thing
  Upon the dull earth dwelling.
To her garlands let us bring!
SHAKSPERE.

ACT I

Scene First. [*The Prologue.*]

[*A room in Hollis Hall, Harvard College. The room is furnished tastefully. A drop-light descends upon a table in the centre. On the table lies tumbled manuscript. Felix, in his college gown, is walking back and forth. He stops to lift a sheet of the manuscript.*]

FELIX

Act Fourth, and how to end it! This comedy of mine is turning tragic. But, no! He must not win her. Why, he's the villain, not the hero. And yet — to be true to life. I must be true — with splendid realism, as the critics say — to the falsity of human nature. Yet I am human, Mr. Realist, even as you. Then — how say you! — let's be false to our own falsity, and true to something — better, we will call it. I'll do it.

[*Scratches a line across the manuscript.*]

There, Sandrac! There's a sword-thrust for you, even in the middle of your wedding scene.

[*Throws away the pen.*]

That's done, thank God! But now — how to end it all with truth? Dear Sylvia, only you can help me now.

[*He starts and listens. Outside, loud noises — laughter, singing and stamping — draw near.*]

Fate and the fellows!

[*Quickly gathering up his manuscript, he writes on a piece of paper, and lays it on the table; then, turning down the gas, he slips, noiselessly, into his bedroom, closing the door.*]

STUDENTS
[*Outside.*]

Cloudsley! Cloudsley! Cloudsley!
Rah, rah, rah!
Rah, rah, rah!
Rah, rah, rah! Cloudsley!
Punch!
We — want — punch!

A HIGH VOICE

Who wants punch?

STUDENTS

We do! — Halloa, Cloudsley!

[*Confused clamor of voices.*]

Turn up the gas. Come out of your nightcap! Lend us a megaphone. Where are you at? Oh, I say!

ANOTHER VOICE (HUGH'S)

Hush, duffers. Here, give me a lift.

[*A murmur outside, and kicks against the door; then Hugh's head appears through the transom.*]

HUGH

Higher! Boost me, mon. Hold on to my hoof, there, Warty. Easy now. Reach me the cane — the cane, I say — damn it, the cane. That's it.

[*From outside, a cane is thrust to Hugh through the transom. With it, he reaches down and pushes the catch-lock within. At the same time, the handle is turned from outside and the door is thrown open. In rushes a crowd of students, in caps and gowns, who turn up the gas and scatter about the room, helping themselves to drink and tobacco.*]

STUDENTS
[*As they enter.*]

Hurray!

WARTON
[*Shouts.*]

What — ho! mine host!

HUGH

[*Who is left stuck in the transom, his legs dangling, midair, in the open doorway.*]

Hold on, fellows! Take me out of this.

[*The students jeer at him.*]

WARTON

[*Who affects a light air of badinage and conscious super-culture.*]

Ah! Merriman, Merriman, such is the snare for him who cometh as a thief by night.

HUGH

Hang your soul, Warty! I'd drop down myself, I tell you, if this cursed rag of mine wasn't caught.

WARTON

Verily, 'tis easier for a camel to pass through the eye —

HUGH

Will any one give me a lift-down, by God?

FIRST STUDENT

Go it, man! make it a touch-down; only one yard to gain. To Hell with Yale! The beers are up.

[*Several students pop bottles and hold them enticingly under Hugh's nose.*]

HUGH

Oh, all right, I can hang here, till the Proctor comes.

STUDENTS

Cheese it. The Proctor.

WARTON

[*Approaching Hugh, warily.*]

Honest Hugh, hadst thou read thy Shakspere with diligence, pardee, thou wouldst have taken profit from thy Grandsire Falstaff, and not have fallen amongst us merry wives. However, for the Proctor's sake —

[*With his pocket-knife, he cuts the strings that hold Hugh, whose gown tears as he falls on his feet to the floor. The rest of the gown remains hanging from the transom.*]

THE PROLOGUE

HUGH
[*Examining his curtailed gown.*]
Gad, fellows, I call this humiliating.

SECOND STUDENT
[*Offering his beer.*]
Here, Merry, don't you care. We came here to initiate Cloudsley; not you.

FIRST STUDENT
Yes; but where *is* Cloudsley?

WARTON
[*Picking up Felix's note.*]
Behold! He hath penned a pronouncement!
[*Reading.*]
"Back in a few minutes. Make yourselves at home. Cloudsley."

[*Warton looks round at the fellows, who are stowing themselves in comfortable chairs and divans, helping themselves to cigars and beer, or making punch.*]

Why hesitate, gentlemen? Make yourselves at home.

SECOND STUDENT
Cert; and as to this initiation?

HUGH
Wait; I'd go slow.

WARTON
And why, prithee?

FIRST STUDENT

Yes, what's struck you, Merriman? Cloudsley has had a cinch all the year — never took his initiation. We other fellows had to stand it. Why shouldn't he?

HUGH

He's different.

WARTON

Rot!

HUGH

Well —

WARTON

Well, what?

HUGH

Fellows, I've bunked with Cloudsley. When I was sick at midyears, he took me in here and fairly coddled me.

WARTON

Ergo, *we* must coddle him now, eh?

HUGH

Well, I saw him days, and I heard him talk in his sleep nights, and I tell you, fellows, Cloudsley's in love.

[*The room bursts into roars of laughter.*]

WARTON

In love! Oho! Cupid, hast thou shot Plato through the Idea!

FIRST STUDENT

What's the girl's name?

HUGH

Sylvia; and I tell you, Cloudsley's got it bad. Why, he writes verses to her, I guess. Anyway, he'll walk up and down in a mighty eloquent silence, muttering like Hamlet. And then, by Gad, for all like Hamlet, you'd think he saw a ghost, for he'll call out "Sylvia!" to the empty air, and swear by his soul, he'll save her from her lover.

SECOND STUDENT

The poor duff must have been jilted.

HUGH

Damme, I think that's it. I spoke to him about it once, but he smiled and tried to stuff me. "Sylvia?" says he, "why, man, she's just a character in a play I'm writing." And then he laughed at me, but he walked away mighty sober.

WARTON

A character in a play? So Cloudsley writes plays, does he?

HUGH

Lordy, yes; all sorts o' queers. But say, as for Sylvia — well! You know, I *may* be a good grab-bag for taffy, but he couldn't shove that down me. A fellow don't stay awake nights, nor forget to go to dinner, nor talk moonshine at noon, just because he's *interested* in a *character* of a *play* he's writing. It takes more than that, I can tell you, by experience. It takes a bloomin' fine girl!

WARTON

Dare say! But what has Cloudsley's being in love got to do with this initiation?

[*Reënter Felix, unobserved.*]

HUGH

Why, just this: there isn't going to be any initiation.

WARTON

Who's going to prevent it?

HUGH

Me. I tell you, damn it, I'm dead stuck on Felix, and for the short and long of it, if any man wants to initiate him now, he's got to settle with me first.

FELIX

[*Stepping forward.*]

And what will you do to the initiator, Hugh?

HUGH

Halloa, Felix, you here?

WARTON

Hail, Signore Felice Nuvoloso! Make yourself at home.

FELIX

[*With a mock bow.*]

Grazie, Eccelenza! But first, I believe, I must "settle" with Hugh here.

HUGH

Damn it, these fellows —

FELIX

Are about to confer upon me the honor of an initiation. Am I right?

FIRST STUDENT

That's the size of it.

HUGH

But I say —

FELIX

That nothing can exceed my boundless gratitude. 'Tis a privilege, believe me, I have long sighed for.

THIRD STUDENT

Hear! Hear!

HUGH

Come off! — You mean you want to be initiated? — straight?

FELIX

With all the gravity of the grave. What, Hugh! Would you have me exempted from an honor conferred upon all the rest of you? —

[*With a flourish.*]

Classmates, I am your grateful servant. Your quest with me this night has affected my feelings deeply. Believe me, to bestride the goat of our fraternity would stir my heart-pulse with a more perspiring ardor than to mount the pommel of Pegasus. Nothing, in short, to-night would more fire my soul than this initiation, if alas! —

[*He smiles.*]
— I were not otherwise engaged.
[*Stamping, jeering and groaning.*]

FIRST STUDENT

Say, fellows, catch on to the " engaged."

THIRD STUDENT

Hear! Hear!

STUDENTS

What's her name ? — *Sylvia ?*

FELIX

Why, yes, Sylvia was the lady with whom —

WARTON

Oho! Is she here?
[*With a slurring smile.*]
Gad, fellows, we'd best be out of this.
[*Bows away.*]
Cloudsley, a thousand pardons for intruding.

FELIX

[*Looking Warton in the eye.*]

Hold on, Warton. Not for the intrusion, but for the inference — I'll take your thousand pardons. Are they mine?

WARTON

[*Cringingly.*]
Oh, your humble servant!

FELIX

Hugh, show these Bacchantes how to mix punch.

HUGH

I'm their man.

[*To a student.*]

Hand me the mint and mandarin there. But say, Felix, I'm glad you've owned up: tell us about her. Who is Sylvia, anyhow, and what's her last name?

FELIX

Why, the name of the last happy thought in your heart.

HUGH

[*Aside to Warton.*]

Told you so, Warty. Clean off.

[*To the others.*]

Well, every man to his taste. A fig, say I, for these girls in the thought; give me one in the flesh.

[*Raising his glass.*]

Fellows, here's to our sweethearts, and to every honest girl that can weigh down a buggy spring.

FELIX

[*Drinking with the others.*]

To the belle of the buggy spring!

SECOND STUDENT

Here's a bumper to her!

THIRD STUDENT

Song! Song!

FIRST STUDENT

"Johnny Harvard!" — Join in, boys!
[*A knock sounds on the door, but is not heard by them. All sing vociferously. Hugh stirs the bowl in time to the music, and Felix thrums the guitar.*]

ALL

"Oh! here's to Johnny Harvard,
  Fill him up a full glass,
  Fill him up a glass to his name and fame.
  And at the same time
  Don't forget his true love,
  Fill her up a bumper to the brim;
  Drink, drink, drink,
  Fill her up a bumper to the brim."
[*Amid the shouts and self-applause that immediately follow, enter Mr. Berry and Mr. Rourke.*]

STUDENTS

[*In confused cry.*]

Come in! Come in! A rouser for the old bucks!
Rah, rah, rah!
Rah, rah, rah!
Rah, rah, rah!
Old Bucks!

FELIX

[*Remonstrating.*]

Fellows! — Come in, Mr. Berry, come in.

MR. BERRY

The door being ajar, Felix, and our knockings unheard, we —

MR. ROURKE

[*Stepping to the punch-bowl, speaks with a slight brogue.*]

We walked in, sir, to join your wake.

BERRY

[*Buttonholing Felix.*]

Old friend of mine — actor — brought him round to hear your play.

STUDENTS

[*Surrounding Rourke with raised glasses.*]

A toast to Irish! Speech — speech!

ROURKE

Gentlemen, I drink with ye to the health and spirits o' the fond departed.

[*Laughter, with shouts of —* "Who? — the Proctor?"]

FELIX

Fellows, a word with you.

STUDENTS

Hear! Hear!

FELIX

In remembering the Proctor, remember your degrees this week.

HUGH

Gad, yes; let up, boys.

FIRST STUDENT

[*Mounting a chair.*]

Here's to the Proctor — three cheers and a Tiger.

STUDENTS

Hish! Hish! Pull him down.

FIRST STUDENT

Down front!

BERRY

Rourke, this is my boy, Felix Cloudsley.

FELIX

Mr. Rourke —

ROURKE

Mr. Cloudsley, it gives me real pleasure to drink to your good health.

FELIX

I hope, Mr. Rourke, you will pardon —

ROURKE

[*Smiling.*]

Pardon! Why, bless ye, sir, you could double the price of admission and make your fortune.

[*Helping himself to punch again.*]

By your leave, Mr. Cloudsley —

FELIX

Please.

[*To Berry.*]

This is mighty good of you to come. I have a great deal to ask you —

WARTON

[*Who has beckoned the students aside mysteriously.*]

You understand, the masks and togs are in my room, at the end of the corridor.

[*Loudly.*]

— Come on!

FELIX

Drop in again, fellows.

FIRST STUDENT

Never you fear.

[*Stealthily pushing back the door catch, speaks to Warton.*]

The catch-lock is open.

THIRD STUDENT

[*Singing.*]

"Sweet Marie, come to me! Come to me, Sweet Marie."

WARTON

[*To Felix.*]

Till the witching hour!

[*Then stealing tiptoe toward Rourke and making a mystical gesture, he murmurs with a very broad brogue.*]

" Soft you now! — the fair Ophelia!"

ROURKE

[*Turns quickly, seizes Warton by the nape of the neck with one hand, and makes a theatrical gesture of supplication with the other.*]

"Nymph! In thy orisons be all my sins remembered!"

[*Then seizing him also by the seat of his trousers, he runs Warton out of the room. Felix and Berry applaud, with laughter.*]

FELIX

I see you've not forgotten your cues, Mr. Rourke.

ROURKE

No, sir; I once performed the noble Dane myself, and I'll hear no aspersions cast on his American accent.

FELIX

You fit new business to the old lines.

ROURKE

And that, sir, is the actor's prerogative. The actor is the soul and substance of the lines. Without his body's breath, what would they be? Why, words, sir; as the immortal Prince hath it: "words, words, words."

BERRY

Slowly, Rourke! Are we to understand you that the soul and substance of Shakspere are in stage production?

ROURKE

[*Taking a pipe and seating himself.*]

Is it Shakspere's plays ye mean, or his poems?

FELIX

Aren't they one and the same?

ROURKE

Me boy! Me boy! Ye're young yet.
[*Reaching his pipe across to Berry's cigar.*]
Give us a light, Berry, man.

BERRY

Give us a light on your argument.

ROURKE

Yourself, too? Well! Poems is poems; plays is plays. Don't mix 'em. That's all.

FELIX

But which do you consider the truer to life?

ROURKE

The truer, is it? Well, now you've got me. For the difference between a play and a poem, so to speak, is the difference between a white lie and a whopper.

FELIX

[*Laughing.*]

How's that?

ROURKE

Faith, I'm not joking at all. A dramatist is a liar by necessity; but a poet is a liar by choice. Sure, at least, a dramatist *tries* to speak the truth, and it's no fault of his if his play, by its nature as an imitation of real life, is but a make-believe after all. His object anyhow is to stick close to that real life, like a man. But a poet — on my heart, he's a deal worse of a duffer, for he'll lie like a Frenchman by the hour, and the devil-a-bit he cares, except to make the one lie prettier than t'other.

FELIX

But, Mr. Rourke, what if a play should contain poetry?

ROURKE

'Twould be a sad contamination. I can think of no other cure but to draw the bad blood out, or to amputate the poetic part. But, Mr. Cloudsley, 'tis yourself are the student; and as to being a metaphysical professor — alas for the profession! I neglected it in my boyhood. If I might suggest, then, mightn't we hear a bit of this play of your own, sir, which my friend Berry has spoken to me about, as being, he said, a promising piece, sir?

[*Tapping his head.*]

We could then discuss these matters less in the nebular hypothesis.

BERRY

That's right, Felix, — your play.

FELIX

Excuse me a minute. I will get it.

[*Exit to his bedroom.*]

BERRY

Well, what do you think of him?

ROURKE

A nice boy, and his punch is out of sight.

THE PROLOGUE

BERRY

I knew his parents intimately. Since they died, I have kept a kind of wing over him. He hasn't been at all well lately, and I'm anxious.

ROURKE

Bless his heart! He should take a week's run of one night stands, and brush off the cobwebs o' classicism.

BERRY

I hardly think that would serve. His malady appears to be mental. This play of his — a piece of some talent, though extravagantly youthful — seems to absorb his mind, and set him off in the wildest of speculations as to the relation of life to his imagination. The imagination, he believes, is a faculty of perception and creation. So, on the one hand, his imagination can perceive truths beyond mere eyesight; and on the other, it can create, from these truths, beings beyond mere flesh and blood — creatures which are henceforth indestructible, immortal; for whose existence he himself is responsible, as the good Lord for him. Why, man, he believes it; but what's worse, it's making him ill.

ROURKE

The boy has overstudied. He should see a doctor.

BERRY

I think he should. And yet, Rourke, I'm not so certain that our doctors, or we other practical old fellows of experience, can determine always where higher sensibility ends and aberration begins. Anyway, the doctors themselves would agree that we must meet Felix on his own ground.

ROURKE

Leave him to me, — bless him! If I don't rub the common sense into his sensibility, call me an Irishman.

BERRY

I will, Rourke. Blarney the boy and I'll bless you! Yet not *too* Irish with him. I haven't told you the worst yet.

ROURKE

Eh? What's got him worse than Imagination?

BERRY

Love!

ROURKE

In the heart, is it? or the hat?

BERRY

Rourke, be sober. You may guess how far gone he is, when I tell you that he has actually fallen in love with one of the characters in his own play.

ROURKE

[*Staring.*]

No, by St. Patrick! Poor boy! Poor boy! And him too living in such jolly apartments as this. Well, here's a health to's sweetheart — the Virgin save her!

THE PROLOGUE

[*Ladling more punch and humming.*]
"Let the toast pass,
Drink to the lass,
I'll warrant she'll prove an excuse for the glass."

[*Reënter Felix, with a manuscript. At the same moment, through a tapestry which hangs on the wall opposite him, appears, in faint light, the figure of a girl. She makes toward Felix a gesture of pathetic appeal, seeming to beseech him for his manuscript; then disappears.*]

FELIX

[*Starting forward.*]

Stay! — Sylvia!
[*He pauses in the middle of the room, moved, oblivious of the others.*]

BERRY

[*Hurrying to him.*]
What is it?

FELIX

There! — Gone again.

ROURKE

In God's name, man, what ails ye?

BERRY

Bring some wine.

ROURKE

[*Patting Felix on the shoulder, offers him his glass of punch.*]
There, there, my boy; a bit of a swallow will fix ye up.

FELIX

Thanks, no. You saw nothing? But of course not.

BERRY

You're not well, Felix. Take my word; these are hallucinations.

FELIX

Hallucinations! Why, yes; that's the name psychologists give them, and study them in laboratories. But is not love an hallucination? Are not beauty, truth, ideality, hallucinations too? Do they not take on forms at midday and mock us — for they die?

BERRY
[*Gently.*]

Felix—

FELIX

My kind friend —

BERRY

I beg of you —

FELIX
[*Quickly.*]

Do you believe in fairies?

BERRY

Fairies?

FELIX

Do you believe in water-nymphs and fauns, in sylvan creatures, such as the Greeks worshipped, before ever Empedocles put clockwork in the world?

BERRY

What — supernatural beings?

FELIX
No, natural.

BERRY
[*Smiling.*]
Fairies of flesh and blood?

FELIX
No, for so they would not be fairies.

BERRY
Why, what do you mean, then? I believe such creatures exist merely in fancy.

FELIX
Exactly — where we all exist. Thank you.

ROURKE
Faith, you're welcome, my boy. And now take a smack of the punch, just to warm up your superior apperceptions.

FELIX
[*Smiles faintly, then laughs.*]
Forgive me. Isn't it pitiful — what a fool a little laughter can make of a man? The tragic heart has perfect key; but screw it a bit in the ribs, and crack! It's sharp or flat — part of the common discord.
[*Drinks the proffered punch.*]

ROURKE
And that's right. A man's head is the balloon of his fancy, and in it he makes many heavenly excursions. But, boy, he must stow sufficient ballast in

the stomach, or else — good-by to the earth! He'll sail away up, clean through the gate o' St. Peter.

FELIX

What a calamity that would be!

ROURKE

It would indeed, sir. To intrude upon the propriety of the angels is not decent in a modest man. Your health, sir.

BERRY

[*Touching his glass to Rourke's.*]
And success to "Sylvia!"
[*They sit.*]

ROURKE

"Sylvia?" — The name of his play, is it?

FELIX

Partly; the play is called — "A Garland to Sylvia."

ROURKE

A poor name altogether; it's not catchy. Call the girl Peggy and drop the Garland.

BERRY

Rourke, you're incorrigible.

[*Rourke gives a solemn sign to Berry and then a wink.*]

FELIX

Shall I begin?

BERRY

Do. By the way, when did you finish it?

FELIX

I haven't finished it.

BERRY

Haven't? What troubles you?

FELIX

[*Smiling.*]

The ending.

BERRY

I hope you're not still worrying over your moral right to make your characters what you please.

FELIX

Maybe I am, for I want them to be true.

BERRY

But, dear boy, what has truth to do with art?

FELIX

Or art with moral right, you would say!

BERRY

Precisely: the best morality may be the worst of art.

FELIX

Yes, and the worst morality — may it be the best of art?

ROURKE

Faith, tis the *only* kind, sir! Fine art is like fine cheese: 'tis not in good taste till it smells.

[*Winking across at Berry.*]

I see you're no connyshur, sir.

FELIX

[*Musing.*]

So you think that in my play —

ROURKE

Your play, is it! Ah, now, that's not a matter of good taste, but good business. Serve your public a fine moral, of course. But the main thing is — has your play got action? Keep your actors hustling; acting, sir, acting; what else are they for? Keep your audience staring. Startle 'em, sir. Make the men forget their bank accounts, and the women their dressmakers. That's the test of a play, sir.

FELIX

I agree with you heartily. But may I ask a question? We may forget our money troubles, you know, by gazing at a sunset, or we may forget them by having our corns trod on. Now just which means of oblivion, may I ask, do you intend here?

ROURKE

Sunsets, sir, don't divert a man's thoughts from his troubles. I never saw one yet, but I wondered whether 'twould rain or not for the evening's performance. But the play, sir: show us your play.

FELIX

[*Handing it.*]

This is the manuscript.

THE PROLOGUE

BERRY

Read it yourself, Felix. Your Dramatis Personæ.

FELIX

[*Reads.*]

A Garland to Sylvia. Characters —Men: Sandrac, an Oxford Student of Astrology and Magic.

ROURKE

Of what, sir?

FELIX

Magic.

ROURKE

What sort of a plot are you giving us?

FELIX

A fairy tale.

ROURKE

Pish!

[*Berry makes a sign of moderation to Rourke, who relights his pipe and twinkles at him.*]

FELIX

[*Reads.*]

Sandrac —

ROURKE

The hero, is he?

FELIX

Yes.

[*Reads.*]

Babblebrook, a courtier; Ishmael Sob, a curate; Pierre, a painter; Alberto, a violinist.

ROURKE

Pish, sir, pish!

FELIX
[*Reads.*]
Hikrion, a woodcutter, foster-father of Sylvia. Women: —

ROURKE
Stop a bit. Which is your villain?

FELIX
I read his name, I think: Sandrac.

ROURKE
But you said he's the hero.

FELIX
So he is.

ROURKE
[*Chuckling.*]
Ay, then, Berry, look sharp. Read on, read on.

FELIX
[*Reads.*]
Women characters: Sylvia —

ROURKE
The star, I presume.

FELIX
As you wish.
[*Reads.*]
Fervian, Flurriel, Fresca, her handmaids; six others of her handmaids; wooers; spirits —

ROURKE
What's that? — spirits? No, no, m' boy. That's too heavy on the property man. Ghost skirts and

THE PROLOGUE

moonlight come high. Turn 'em off; they'll lose you twenty per cent.

FELIX
Thanks; I'll note that also.

[*Reads.*]

Act First, Scene: The Forest of Arden.

ROURKE
Arden! Ha! Poaching in Willie's woods!

FELIX
Willie himself was a poacher.

[*Reads.*]

Act I.

I must explain to you that, as the curtain rises, it is early dawn in the forest. For the first moment or two nothing is heard but the echoing strokes of a woodcutter; then, from different directions, are heard two voices calling behind the scene.

[*Reads*]

FIRST VOICE
Woodchopper, ho!

SECOND VOICE
Woodchopper, ho!

[*Enter Babblebrook; his courtier's dress is tattered with thorns: he walks limply and looks worn and sleepy.*]

ROURKE
He's alone on the stage?

FELIX
Yes, the curate hasn't entered yet.
[*Reads.*]

BABBLEBROOK
       So this is
The wood of Arden — would I were home!
[*Shouts.*]
        Which way,
Good Master Woodchopper?

THE SECOND VOICE
[*Calling.*]
    Which way?

BABBLEBROOK
[*Shivering.*]
        Snakes' hisses!
Voices! Enchantment! Did it answer, eh?
How! Did it mock? The wood is voluble
With kisses as an unlit alcove. I
Shall be enzoned with nymphs, and made a gull,
A rape of.
  [*Driving off a swarm of mosquitoes.*]
   Shee! They cluster now. Fie! Fie!
As thick as grapes on Bacchus. Oh, their stings,
Their pepper-pinchings and their back-bites, sly
As ladies' tongues. Hence! Hush your pipey wings,
Ye gnats and knaves!
    [*Babblebrook kneels.*]

You understand, Mr. Rourke, to the audience the scene is still half dark.

ROURKE

To me, it's dark entirely.

FELIX

[*Reads.*]

O courteous, kingly Sun,
If ever thou didst smile on mortal things
Oh, smile on 'em now! If ever thou wert known
To rise in the morning, get up now! This day
Break not thy golden rule. Thy will be done!

[*He rises. Enter Sob; neither sees the other.*]

BOTH

[*Calling together.*]

Who's there?

SOB

A voice!

BABBLEBROOK

A nymph!

SOB

O Lord, which way?

BABBLEBROOK

I will not be seduced; no, though it be
Circe herself.

[*He steps on a stick, which cracks; alarmed, he draws his sword.*]

BOTH

[*Calling together.*]

Ho, woodchopper!

[*A loud knock at Felix's door.*]

ROURKE

Faith, there he comes now — chopping the door down!

FELIX
[*Calls.*]

Come in!

[*Enter the Proctor.*]

THE PROCTOR

Lights out, Mr. Cloudsley.

FELIX

Lights out! — at this hour?

PROCTOR

It's near midnight.

FELIX

Isn't this stretching a rule?

PROCTOR

I have reason for suspecting disorderly conduct here to-night. You will have the goodness to make all dark and quiet at once. Good night.

[*Exit.*]

ROURKE
[*Jumping up.*]

The Proctor, is it?

FELIX

Yes.

ROURKE

Faith, then, we'll have him in.

[*Slips to the door, and calls into the corridor.*]

Your honor!

PROCTOR
[*Outside.*]

What's wanted?

ROURKE

The ecstasy of your society by the flowing bowl of Hollis.

PROCTOR

Lights out, I said!

ROURKE

[*Returning.*]

Bedad, then, Mr. Cloudsley, we must even be quitting your hospitality.

FELIX

I am truly sorry, though it gives you, sir, a fortunate chance of escape.

ROURKE

Not a bit, m' boy! The punch might have been worse; but I'll grant ye the play might 'a' been better. And with that take my humble advice: don't run a stage "elevator." Stick to the ground-floor and catch the customers.

BERRY

Don't let this disturb you, Felix. It's just as well, for you need the sleep.

ROURKE

[*Shaking Felix's hand.*]

Good night, lad. May ye keep as lively as your punch. God bless ye!

FELIX

Good night, sir. Can you see the way?

[*To Berry, pressing his hand.*]

Good night.

[*Closing the door, he turns out the gas, and stands in the firelight.*]

People are kind, yet, except for kindness, so far sundered! My dearest friend stands on the far horizon of my soul, whose brim ever widens before me, as I run to reach it. Ah, I'm heart-weary and perplexed. To finish the act — the play — to end all truly! Put this Sandrac in my Sylvia's arms? God curse him, no! What to do, then? But first, what's true! What's true?

[*He takes up his guitar and thrums it faintly, with pauses.*]

Could Sylvia love him? Take him to her heart? Could such a union be and heaven allow it? No! Yet he alone has won her; for only he of all has guessed her secret worth, and she has promised her heart to him who shall guess it. Yet how could she have thought — have fancied even — that such a heart as his could construe her beauty, and still cherish its own ugliness; could seek her love, only for selfish rapture; could emulate her truth, only for self-laudation? Yet Sandrac does so, and wins. Or, *seems* to win? Which? Which? I'm soul-sick with the thought.

[*Sitting in front of the dying fire, he sings to his guitar.**]

Who is Sylvia? What is she,
   That all her swains commend her?
Holy, fair and wise is she:
   The heaven such grace did lend her
That admirèd she might be.

Is she kind as she is fair?
   For beauty lives with kindness.
To her eyes love doth repair,
   To help him of his blindness,
And being helped, inhabits there.

[*While he sings the second verse,* SYLVIA *enters, as before, through the wall tapestry. Noiselessly she crosses to Felix, and is about to touch his manuscript, when he turns dreamily and looks at her.*]

Sylvia!

   [*She glides to the wall; he follows, supplicating.*]

Do not leave me! Speak to me — one word that I may believe I am not mad. Tell me he is not true — Sandrac. Tell me he is not true. Oh, if you love me, speak!

SYLVIA

   [*Pointing to the manuscript.*]
Destroy him.
   [*She disappears.*]

FELIX

Gone! But she loves me. Still Sylvia loves me! Sandrac, you hear? "Destroy him." Ah, now it's

   * The music to the song is that of Schumann.

plain as day. My world is overturned. My play — the fire — my manuscript! They're false, these lovers, and Sandrac falsest of all. In the fire!

[*Snatching his manuscript from the table, he tears it and throws it in the fire; then blows the flame with the bellows.*]

Hearth — be my heart! Heat, be hell itself! Flames, you are love, love, love! It burns, it burns! There you go, Babblebrook, Alberto, Sob — and you, you, Sandrac, my changeling soul, all — all in the fire! At last, they die — now they have passed from me utterly. "Destroy him!" Now it is done! Sandrac dead — and Sylvia loves me —

[*Burying his face in his arms, he sobs.*]

Dear God! Joy is such sweet grief!

[*Enter at back, the Students, in masks and long gowns of white and crimson. Each figure carries a lighted candle. They enter, single file, and surround Felix, who — buried in his own feelings — does not see them.*]

WARTON

[*Nudges Hugh, who is the leader of the pageant; all speak in whispers.*]

Now, Merriman!

HUGH

Curse it, man, I haven't the heart to.

WARTON

Twaddle! — he said he sighed for the privilege.

[*Hugh coughs to attract Felix's attention. The Second Student pokes Hugh in the ribs, whereat the others give sound to stifled giggling.*]

SECOND STUDENT

Go it, Grand Mogul!

HUGH
[*Whispers.*]

Quit, will you?

[*He coughs again. Felix raises his head, and looks at the masked figures, all of whom raise their candles in their right hands, and, stooping, stare at him.*]

FELIX
[*Murmurs.*]

The initiation! Now?

[*They beckon with their candles. Felix rises, smiling.*]

Mysterious gentlemen, you are welcome.

[*He makes a mock reverence, and they bow in return.*]

I hope you enjoyed a pleasant passage on the Styx?

WARTON
[*At Hugh's ear.*]

Speech now, Sir Pluto.

HUGH
[*In a loud whisper.*]

Shut up, Warty.

[*Hugh waves with his candle, Felix follows him to the chair in front of the fire.*]

FELIX

That way, your reverence? I await your commands. What, must I sit? — Nay, gentlemen, after you. You are my guests.

[*The maskers nudge one another, tittering; then — all together — repeat Hugh's gesture to be seated.*]
You insist? Why, then, if that's the fashion in Hades,
[*Sitting, he addresses Hugh, and points to the fire.*]
won't you sit opposite there, and be comfortable?
[*The students snicker again. Hugh signs to two maskers, who come forward, bind Felix's eyes with a handkerchief, and tie him to the chair. This done, the whole crowd of students gather round Felix in a hubbub of whispers. Hugh motions silence and commences in a deep bass voice.*]

HUGH

O Felix, felicissime hominum, tibi ferimus —

FIRST STUDENT
[*Nudging Hugh.*]

Sst! What's that?
[*Hugh pauses. The students listen. Hugh resumes.*]

HUGH

— tibi ferimus et gloriam et —
[*The door opens suddenly; the Proctor enters.*]

PROCTOR

Gentlemen!

STUDENTS
[*Scrambling.*]

Lights out! Lights out!
[*They blow out their candles.*]

THE PROLOGUE

PROCTOR

What is the meaning of this?

STUDENTS

The Proctor!

WARTON

Mum, there!

HUGH

Hist, Warty; this way!

[*The students, jostling the Proctor, scurry off through the corridor.*]

PROCTOR

Gentlemen, this is disgraceful. This shall be reported.

[*Exit.*]

[*The sound of their receding footsteps grows faint and ceases. Felix struggles to rise.*]

FELIX

Tied — blindfold — tied! How silent — and how black!
What does it matter! Now behind these bands,
Imagination, which was Milton's lamp,
Shall be my candle, and light my muse to build
A strong, illustrious theatre in the dark —
This dark, which is the dawn of reverie.
The building-place is cleared; the refuse past
Is swept away; nothing obstructs me now.
Sandrac is dead and Sylvia loves me. — Now!

[*The fire flickers out into* DARKNESS.[1]]

[1] The curtain does not fall.

A GARLAND TO SYLVIA

SCENE SECOND. Act I *of* "*The Reverie.*"
[*Out of the darkness sounds the echoing stroke of an axe; dimly in gradual dawn the outlines of a forest scene grow visible. Felix is then discernible. His chair has turned to the gnarled root of a great tree, beneath which he sits pensive, motionless as an image. His gown has turned gray and his whole appearance misty. Beside him stands an Aged Figure, majestic, cloaked, and still. Where the hearth-fire shone before, now shimmers a nest of glow-worms. Outside, the strokes of the axe sound more loud; then, echoing through the wood — two voices, calling.*]

FIRST VOICE
Woodchopper, ho!

SECOND VOICE
Woodchopper, ho!

[*Enter Babblebrook; his courtier's dress is tattered with thorns, he walks limply and he looks worn and sleepy.*]

BABBLEBROOK
So this is
The wood of Arden — would I were home!
[*Shouts.*]
Which way,
Good Master Woodchopper?

SECOND VOICE
[*Calling.*]
Which way?

BABBLEBROOK
[*Shivering.*]
Snakes' hisses!
Voices! Enchantment! Did it answer, eh?

How? Did it mock? The wood is voluble
With kisses as an unlit alcove. I
Shall be enzoned with nymphs, and made a gull,
A rape of.
        [*Driving off a swarm of mosquitoes.*]
        Shee! They cluster now. Fie! fie!
As thick as grapes on Bacchus. O their stings,
Their pepper-pinchings and their back-bites, sly
As ladies' tongues! Hence! Hush your pipey wings,
Ye gnats and knaves!
        [*Babblebrook kneels.*]
        O courteous, kingly Sun,
If ever thou didst smile on mortal things,
O smile on 'em now! If ever thou wert known
To rise in the morning, get up now! This day
Break not thy golden rule. Thy will be done!
     [*He rises. Enter Sob; neither sees the other.*]

              BOTH
            [*Calling together.*]
Who's there?
              SOB
        A voice!

            BABBLEBROOK
        A nymph!

              SOB
                        O Lord, which way?

            BABBLEBROOK
I will not be seduced;   no, though it be
Circe herself.
[*He steps on a stick, which cracks; alarmed, he draws his
            sword.*]

BOTH
[*Calling together.*]
Ho, woodchopper!
[*Both recoil and pray. Outside, the axe resounds again, and in the intervals of its strokes, a strange voice, ranging from basso to falsetto, sings.*]

THE VOICE
A hard hand and a hove hand, ho!
  Maketh the big oak bend.
The monarch that sitteth so grand, ho!
  Leans to a lowly end.
With high and low of every kind,
Old Death he hath an axe to grind.
  God give us grace to mend!

BABBLEBROOK
    It fades.
Where is the voice?
[*Outside the axe-stroke ceases; a shrill warning cry is heard; then a loud crack and whirr of foliage, as a tall tree falls thundering in the background. Babblebrook and Sob, rushing wildly to escape its fall, run accidentally into each other's arms.*]

BABBLEBROOK
Help!

SOB
Help!
[*Sob clings convulsively to Babblebrook, who, in a frenzy of fear, extricates himself.*]

BABBLEBROOK
Off, Echo-nymph! — Sham!

Back! I'm no innocent; I'm a devil of blades.
I know the skirt-tribe to their shoe-lacings.
Begone; I'm old in the art; you cannot cram
Me.

SOB

Gentle woodman, are you he that sings
In the forest?

BABBLEBROOK

"Woodman?" "Woodman!" Sylph, 'tis true
That I have supped with princes, dined with kings,
Yet now am "woodman." Nut-brown is my hue!
I am thy faun, Diana.

[*Attacking Sob fiercely.*]

Drink the dregs
Of love and death, which —

[*Pausing wonderstruck.*]

Lady Alicia! who
Are you?

SOB

No nymph; a modest man, who begs
Your grace: a curate, sir, in misery.

BABBLEBROOK

Thank God!

SOB

How, sir?

BABBLEBROOK

Those skirts about your legs
Played false; but Heaven be praised you are a *he*.

[*Embraces Sob.*]

Your name, palpable modest man!

SOB

Ishmael Sob. Sob, sir;

BABBLEBROOK
[*With a sweeping bow.*]
        And mine's Sir Balliol
Babblebrook — by the sex surnamed "Sanscœur."
And now, friend Ishmael, let us end our stroll
In peace; 'tis time I sought my destination;
I am a lover.

SOB
        So am I, my lord.

BABBLEBROOK
"My lord:" lip-loving, luscious deliquation!
Speak it again.

SOB
        My lord —

BABBLEBROOK
                O sugar'd word!
It melts.

SOB
        My lord, I love —

BABBLEBROOK
                Peace, fool! You'll smother
All the nine Muses with your ignorance.
You are too fleshly. I am quite another
Sort. I am kiss-accoutred. I'm Romance
Anthropomorphized! Your miasmic moons
And midnight are my *forte*. I like this dance
In the underbrush — rather. For the starry boons
Of a lady's eyes, I plunge into the briers,
And range the wood for lions; read the runes

Of rotted stumps for mushrooms (Romance requires
A stomach, and the stomach seeks base earth),
And thus, by knightly quests, I fan the fires
Of my fierce love for Sylvia, and her worth.

      SOB
     [*Sighing.*]
And so do I!
      BABBLEBROOK
    Thou liest!
      SOB
        Sheathe thy blade,
My lord! Heaven witness that I ne'er spoke mirth
I' my life. This Sylvia whom I seek's a maid
Who makes her rustic dwelling in this wood
With her old foster-father. Yet, 'tis said,
Though she is shy, she comes of as gentle blood
As any lady rides in London.

      BABBLEBROOK
       Zounds!
'Tis she. Speak: is she rich?

      SOB
       She must have treasure;
Vast treasure, too, my lord, for there's good grounds
To guess she's royalty, whom high displeasure
Has hid in this far forest.

      BABBLEBROOK
      And you think,
Miscreant curate, she would have thee?

      SOB
        Please your
Lordship, 'tis like she does not know the link

To her birth, being found a babe; but after all,
Even if she does, from *me* she should not shrink,
For man is man — a noble animal.

BABBLEBROOK

True, hag; but not in shameless petticoats
Like thine. I'll show thee *man*.
[*Plunges at him with his sword, striking far off the mark, but terrifying Sob.*]

Base curate, fall!
Fight! Flee! Fade! This is *man*. Man slives the throats
That speak profane praise of his mistress' face;
Exhale, then! — Soft! If you be dead and gone,
I'll be alone in this nymph-haunted place.
[*Extending his arms, with a smile.*]
Ishmael!

SOB

[*As they embrace.*]
'Save you, sir.

BABBLEBROOK

Love's not a bone
To squabble over. Love should cofraternize.
Come!

SOB

Where?

BABBLEBROOK

To Sylvia: for hark, mine own!
There lives a man to damn our enterprise:
A base astrologer, a youth profound
In Alchemy and black art. He's named Sandrac.
He has two acid eyes that peer around
And smile at you, like culprits in the hand-rack.

SOB

Heaven shield us, sir! What of *him*?

BABBLEBROOK

This: he has come
On foot, over dale and down, through wood and sand track,
To find out Sylvia and to take her home
With him.

SOB

What! have you seen him?

BABBLEBROOK

Yes, I cross'd
His path last eve. So hasten! For if we
Be last to Sylvia, Sylvia will be lost
To us, — or what's more apropos, to me.
Ha! Here's our woodman.

[*Enter Hikrion, with an axe, singing.*]

HIKRION

What is strong,
And lasts long,
Sing it a song —
 Cheerily O!

Time, time,
That sits in the slime,
Ring him your rhyme —
 Wearily O!

[*At Hikrion's song, the Aged Figure beside Felix stirs and touches him on the brow. Felix lifts his head, and wakens slowly to conscious attention.*]

BABBLEBROOK

                          Good day, old good fellow.
You pipe up early.

HIKRION

               Ah! Good day to ye,
My pretty masters. Be you two the mellow
Night-birds I heerd coo up the larks o' late?

BABBLEBROOK

How mean you? Birds!

HIKRION

                  Their note was " Hello! Hello! "
A sweet wood-wooing.

BABBLEBROOK

Man!

HIKRION

                      A sing'lar trait;
[*Jerking his thumb at Sob.*]
Ye'll tell the hen-bird by her feathers.

BABBLEBROOK

                           Peasant,
Beware! This worthy gentleman's my pious
Friend. So, beware the birch-stick.

HIKRION

                      Dear, it's pleasant,
To meet with modesty, aren't it?

BABBLEBROOK

                         Zacharias
And Judas! Upstart, I will teach thee whether

The modest mode be taught by swine, or by us
Of better breed.

[*He draws his sword and makes a lunge at Hikrion, who, with
a twinkle, catches it away from him; then examines it,
whistling softly.*]

      HIKRION
    A mighty smart tail feather!
I guess I'll fetch it home to Sylvia.

      BABBLEBROOK
    [*Gasping.*]
        Who?
      HIKRION
I've got a daughter kep' to home. — Fine weather,
Aren't it? Good morning.

      BABBLEBROOK
      Hold! Hold! Take us, too,
Good Hikrion. Art thou not Hikrion,
Her noble father? Stay!

      SOB
      Wait, sir! we woo
Your heavenly daughter —

      BABBLEBROOK
    [*Thrusting Sob aside.*]
        Peace, thou jackass' son! —
O Hikrion, great hermit of the grove!
Far-famèd forester! know, I am one
Who come, uplift like Diomede to Jove,
To sue from thee thy daughter. I admire,
Nay, worship, nay, adore, nay, like, nay, love —
Thy daughter. But I first address her sire,

As doth become Sir Balliol Babblebrook.
Speak! I'm your servant, sir: behold my squire;
Use him for what you will.

     SOB
      Nay, by the Book —

    BABBLEBROOK
     [*To Sob.*]
Hush! Shall we two be rivals?

     HIKRION
      My queer daughter
Catched many a queer fish on her beauty's hook,
But none with such a gill as this. She's caught a
Bull-head here.
    [*To Babblebrook.*]
    So, Sir Diomede, you think
To win my Sylvia?
     SOB
    [*Intervening.*]
   Aye, sir.

    BABBLEBROOK
   [*Pushing Sob away.*]
     I, by sueing
Her noble sire.
     HIKRION
   [*With a sly, knowing glance.*]
    Then let the blind horse wink,
The cat steal cheese, the mice do all the mewing.
[*With a skip and a merry scowl, he peers close in the faces of
    Babblebrook and Sob.*]

Come, masters! By my curls, that look like horns,
Come on! I'll show ye the woodland way o' wooing.
> [*Exit, skipping to his song.*]

> See! the oak
> Turns to smoke
> In chimney choke,
> > Drearily O!

> But peat o' the mire
> Flames in the fire,
> And flies higher —
> > Airily O!

[*During the song, Felix rises and listens as it dies away in the forest.*]
[*Babblebrook and Sob stand staring after Hikrion.*]

BABBLEBROOK

Sob — Sob!

SOB

My lord!

BABBLEBROOK

Lead on!

SOB

The highest born's
The first, my lord.

BABBLEBROOK

Slave! dost thou fear the thorns?

SOB

[*Touching his head.*]

The horns, my lord.

BABBLEBROOK
[*Trembling.*]
The horns?

SOB
He is not made,
Methinks, like common men. He walks uncanny,
And then —
[*Makes the sign again.*]

BABBLEBROOK
[*Drawing close to Sob.*]
What! did you note 'em?

[*They whisper, with timid gestures. Meantime, Felix — leaving the Aged Figure standing by the tree — approaches them, looks them in the eyes, touches their garments. Seeing, however, that they pay no attention to him, he turns pensively away, as if trying to remember.*]

FELIX
What dream is this,
Where thoughts I have written rise up in palpable flesh
And make a ghost of me?

BABBLEBROOK
But he said
That they were curls, not horns.

SOB
Sir! put not any
Trust in his guile.
[*They whisper again. Felix draws nearer.*]

BABBLEBROOK
What, what! His knees? His knees!

SOB

Did not you mark their crook?

[*They whisper again.*]

FELIX

Those words — those words:
"His knees? Did not you mark their crook?" —
   What wind,
Moaned from what muffled cavern of my mind,
Sighs in my ears these sounds?—"His knees!—Did not
You mark their crook?" — Ha, Babblebrook and Sob!
Now, now I know them!

BABBLEBROOK

A satyr of yore?

FELIX

Right; that's right; those are
The very words! He took his cue. Now comes —
"For shame! Such monsters haunt mythologies."

BABBLEBROOK

**For shame! Such monsters haunt mythologies.
Thou slave of superstition, go before!**

SOB

But if —

BABBLEBROOK

I'll have thee hanged for heresies!
[*Sob precedes Babblebrook, and they go.*]

FELIX

[*Following them.*]

Stay!

Stand, elusive shadows! Stop, I say!
'Tis I command you — your creator, Felix. —

[*They disappear in the wood.*]

Gone — gone! Could I not even hold their hems
Between this waterish thumb and forefinger?
What! Is my frame dissolved, like a salt-pillar
In the humid air? Am I a water-wraith
That I should blow through unsubstantial lips
These pale, prismatic bubbles of no sound?
And this intangible wood, where now I walk
Numb-footed, like a friar in the frost, —
What tenebrous dream is this? — Almost I seem
A bodied breeze, for when my pulses beat,
Shrill zephyrs whistle through my reedy veins
And puff my ribs with foam of their own essence.
Yet I am Felix still, and this is Arden,
Where I have wandered many a pensive hour,
Tending my flocks of fancies; ah! but then —
Then — *they* were made of mist as I am now.
Where's Sylvia? She will make me real again
As her own cheek of rose.

[*He crosses toward the right, where* **Sandrac** *enters. The two gowned figures, Sandrac in black, Felix now in misty gray, walk toward each other, till — almost meeting — Felix sees Sandrac, and recoils.*]

Sandrac! O God!

THE REVERIE

SANDRAC[1]

This is the verdurous and virgin shore
Where the wan night-wave heaves its tide of lovers
On odorous dunes, with violets sprinkled o'er;
And here land I, with Sylvia's amorous drovers,
Who are, in love, such umpires of her worth
As cows, in art, are connoisseurs in clovers.
Then well for me, and for the Muses' mirth,
That such they are, for I'll the sooner win
And wed this Sylvia's heaven to my earth.

FELIX

Sandrac, the sophist! He it is, and lives,
Breathes, walks again! I rent him limb from loin,
Tore out his festered heart, dripping with speech,
And cast him headlong all into the fire;
Yet wizard now, like Satan's salamander,
He slips again into the voluble air
And prates of sin, as Socrates of virtue.
Ah God, *I* made him!

[SANDRAC]

A secret Sylvia has: there let's begin.
Sylvia shall keep her secret safe, unless
Some suitor, to her maidenly chagrin,
Shall answer three set questions. If he guess
These right (of which the chief is: " What is she? ")
The lover wins the stakes of loveliness
And Sylvia's treasure's his. Now, let us see:
What is this treasure?

[1] Like Babblebrook and Sob, Sandrac remains totally oblivious of Felix.

FELIX
            'Tis as far from your
Just heritage as heaven from hell's.

            [SANDRAC]
            Is it procurable
By such as I?
            FELIX
                        Yes — God
Forgive me in my ignorance! — for I
Have placed in your apostate hands the key
That unlocks all her shrines.

            [SANDRAC]
            Men think that alchemy
Is my black art, but men are wondrous dull.
For poesie is all my secret power
Which says: Win golden Beauty! Then, never fear it,
The beauteous gold of fame shall be her dower;
Nay more! which tells me Sylvia is —

            FELIX
            Forbear!

            [SANDRAC]
                        A spirit.
            FELIX
                        Curst be
Your knowledge! Curst be I, that taught it you!

            [SANDRAC]
A fairy princess, whom blockheads in bliss
Suppose a princess royal; for they judge
That fairies are but fictions; so they miss
The wealth would give them royal power. But fudge!
I am not of these fools.

FELIX

Would God you were! So you had never aspired
To wrest from Sylvia her throne, and reign
Nero of Arcady. But no! you shall not.
What! In your hand, her sceptre — which is now
A benison of beauty — would become
An engine for all ugliness. Turn back!
Go; I rescind you!

[SANDRAC]

Ah! here's my woodman
Pan, in disguise.

FELIX

Sandrac! — Deaf as the dead!

[*Enter Hikrion, with a willow-switch driving before him Sob and Babblebrook; the latter is laden down by a ponderous weight of logs and brushwood, the former is groaning under the weight of two pails of water, which hang from a yoke on his shoulders.*]

HIKRION

Come, pretty masters, budge!
Sir Diomede, this is the Olympic mood, man;
Your uncle Phœbus woo'd i' the wood way: mark it!
Ksuk! Ksuk!

BABBLEBROOK
[*Groaning.*]

O London!

HIKRION

Budge; we're late; budge.

SANDRAC
[*Calling.*]

Goodman!

[*Hikrion, who is whistling, pays no heed.*]

SOB

Grace, Lord!

HIKRION

Who taps the maple first must bark it;
The sap is Sylvia.

SANDRAC

Goodman, leads this path
To Sylvia's.

HIKRION
[*Turning.*]

Yea, I drive these to her market.
[*Touching up Sob with his switch and clucking with his cheek.*]
Ksuk, Dobbin!

SOB
Grace!

HIKRION

The sinner feels his wrath:
Spare not the rod.
[*To Sandrac.*]

Join you this circus, sir? —
A privilege every suitor of Sylvia hath.

BABBLEBROOK
[*Seeing Sandrac for the first time.*]

Nay, by my lady Alicia, I'll not stir
An inch, if he goes — Satan give him riddance!
I know him for a vile astrologer,
An alchemist. — Kind woodman, give me credence!
First come, first serve.

SANDRAC

[*Bowing, with a sarcastic smile.*]

I pray you, give precedence
To Sylvia's *London* suitors. I will follow.

HIKRION

So be it. Quoth the donkey to the ass:
Come bear a burden! Trol-lee — trollo — trollo!
Nay, quoth the ass, your burden is too bass:
A lighter one is: Hollo — hollo — hollo!

[*Exeunt Hikrion, Sob and Babblebrook. Sandrac pauses a moment, smiling to himself. Felix stands guard over him and, at his first motion to follow the others, steps in his path.*]

FELIX

You shall not pass. For this way Sylvia lies. —

[*Pointing.*]

That way, return!

SANDRAC

How pleasantly a poet's fancies pass!

FELIX

[*Attempting to thrust him back.*]

Stand back! By heaven, no farther!
You think to browbeat *me* too?

[*Sandrac passes on through Felix's arms, as through a mist, and exit in the wood.*]

Ah! I'm naught. —
No, no! Stay your inevitable feet,
Sandrac! — Return! — God help me, I'm weak, weak.

[*He sinks back for support against the gnarled tree. Here the Aged Figure, turning, takes him in his arms. Felix looks in his face with awe.*]

What *are* you?

THE FIGURE

Somnus I am called. This wood
And you are mine.

FELIX

Then hide me in your breast,
For I am faint at heart.

[*Somnus folds Felix in his cloak.*]

[CURTAIN.]

ACT II

ACT II

Scene I: A room in Sylvia's cottage; at back, a great fireplace, within which, on either side, are two stone chimney-seats.

Sylvia and her nine handmaids discovered; Sylvia is playing battledoor and shuttlecock with Flurriel; the others look on, clapping and laughing, except Fervian, who stands aside, watching them pensively.

SYLVIA

Faster!

FRESCA

Brave battledoor!

SYLVIA

Now serve it over
Their heads.

FLURRIEL

[*Striking.*]
There!

SYLVIA

Ho! you box it sidewise, like
A saucy boy.

FLURRIEL

Now, like a naughty lover:
First bandy him, then jilt him; so!

SYLVIA

Fair strike!

FERVIAN
This game, I thought, was shuttlecock, not punning.

SYLVIA
Thy wisdom, girl, like a gray, greedy pike,
Gulps all the twinkling minnows of our funning.
Haha! Well hit!
[*Fervian turns away, hurt.*]

FLURRIEL
[*Panting.*]
Enough!

SYLVIA
Why, Flurriel!
What is the matter?

FLURRIEL
Breath! — My heart is running
Like Daphne, with Apollo at her heel.

SYLVIA
[*Laughs.*]
The fashion of your flesh is too tight-fitting.

FLURRIEL
Would I could let a tuck out!

SYLVIA
So you will
To-night, when we shall all disrobe us, quitting
This mortal millinery. Yet, o' my heart!
I like this garb of Mother Nature's knitting;
'Tis very pretty — mine is — and its art
Is exquisite. Look!

[*Holds out her hand.*]
            Saw you ever a glove
To fit like this? — at once the counterpart
And covering of the spirit! Or know you of
A jewel in the jetted lace of a queen
As bright as Fervian's dark eye, whose love
Darts its own loveliness?

     FERVIAN
            What can it mean?
You call me " greedy pike," and then relent —
Praise my dark eyes!
    SYLVIA
   [*Laughs.*]
            Poor sober-sides! — Why, I'm
A votress at the shrine of merriment,
Where you, a kneeler in this temple of time,
Are scandalized to see my altar scroll'd
With little wingèd jests for cherubim,
Cupids for saints, in chasubles of gold
High chanting shrilly hymns of laughter. Yet,
Sad pilgrim, know, that in this temple old
Are countless shrines; where countless stay their feet
To tell their beads with Aves manifold,
Whilst to one theme both sighs and jests are set —
That's Faith, dear.
    FERVIAN
  [*Embracing her.*]
  Sylvia!

    FLURRIEL
 [*At the window, laughing.*]
    Run, mistress! Run!

THE OTHER HANDMAIDS
What is it?
FLURRIEL
Look!
HANDMAIDS
[*Laughing.*]
O Pan!

FLURRIEL
[*To Sylvia.*]
Run quickly! Hide!

SYLVIA
What's coming? — Why, 'tis only Hikrion.
He's bringing firewood home with his pack-asses.

FLURRIEL
Aye, but the hose-and-doublet fashion
O' the beasts! — the two-legg'd species: — the jack-asses!

FLURRIEL
Nay? Are they mortals? Poor dears! I've a bone
To pick with Hikrion.
[*Enter Hikrion.*]

HIKRION
Here I am back, lasses.
Old Father Early-Worm has catched some birds.

HANDMAIDS
[*Clinging about him.*]
What have you brought us, Pater? Tell, tell, tell!

HIKRION
Peace, pretties; Patience gets the cream o' the curds,
But Fidgets licks the cold spoon.

SYLVIA
                    Sweet dad, —

HIKRION
                              Well,
Sour daughter?
            [*Bowing.*]
            Craving your grace! — Queen Sylvia.

SYLVIA
What have you brought us?

HIKRION
                    Sweets for an epicure:
A blackberry, a raspberry and a
Gooseberry; or, to swap the literature,
A shark, a gold-fish and a porpoise; or
A rook, a parrot and a fatted hen.

SYLVIA
Tut! tut!   We know whom you've been beating, Pater.
      [*Hikrion hangs his head.*]
Your brush-wood could not hide 'em. — They are *men*.

HIKRION
And you can smile?   You make me a maid-hater.
" Ah me," said they, " 'tis all for Sylvia! "   Dear!
Dear! how my heart ached; so I bid 'em wait a
Bit before jogging; but they wouldn't hear
On't.   No, 'twas ever: " Commend us to thy daughter,
The gentle Sylvia! — the tender maiden!
For her our backs are broke; give us more water,
More logs, sweet Hikrion; we are not laden
Enough for gentle Sylvia."

[*With a twinkle and a sudden skip.*]
                    To be shorter,
Have I 'scaped scolding this time?

                    SYLVIA
                              When you're arrayed in
Such wool, old wolf, you'd win Titania.

[*She embraces him with a laugh; he kisses her with a tender humorousness. Flurriel at the door-crack beckons to Fervian.*]

                    FLURRIEL
                                        Sister,
Let's peek.

                    FERVIAN
            [*Approaching curiously.*]
      Fie!

                    FLURRIEL
            Thou'rt afraid?

                    FERVIAN
                              Dost think we can —

[*They peep through the door-chink.*]

                    SYLVIA
When jestings smart, let love go heal the blister.

            [*Spying Fervian and Flurriel.*]

Oh, Doctor Venus! Flurry and Fervian
Have lost their hearts already. So, then! — So!
Reap penance! Each shall have the other's man:

                    [*To Fervian.*]
The courtier's thine;

                    [*Pointing at Flurriel.*]
                    the curate — hers.

FLURRIEL
[*Aside.*]
         Here's woe —
To make wit of.
FERVIAN
Poor swains!
SYLVIA
        Her whom they scan
First, they will take for Sylvia. Therefore show
Them queenly courtesy. But give me Pan
To pipe me wood-songs till the pink o' day.
I'll have no other swain. Come, Hikrion, —
  [*Pulling him by the beard.*]
Come, Mossy-beard, let's cry alack-a-day
To love, and while we dance, sing every one.
[*Sylvia, dancing with Hikrion, who has a blithe skip in his step,
 and the others dancing with them, sing the following song.*]

SYLVIA
If a maiden say thee nay,
Cry to love, Alack-a-day!
 She will alter never
  Never!
 But will still persèver
  Ever!
In her wilful, wilful way.

HIKRION
Therefore, lover, hie thee back;
All thy hopes must go to wrack.
Cry alack, alack, alack!
 Oh, love, alack-a-day!

ALL

Cry, alack-a! lack-a! lack-a!
Lack-a! lack-a-day!

SYLVIA

If a maiden say thee nay,
Lover, cry, alack-a-day!
  She will never, never falter: —
  Not unless her mind should alter
  In a wondrous, wondrous way!

HIKRION

Therefore, maidens, come away!
Crying; Never! nay, nay, nay!
Sighing; Lack a lover ay?·
  Love, O lack-a-day!

ALL

Sighing: Love, I lack a lover;
  Love, O lack-a-day!

[*At the end, Sylvia with her arm about Hikrion dances out, right, with graceful, gay abandon, followed by the others, dancing. Flurriel and Fervian, the last, pause on the edge of the scene.*]

FERVIAN

I the courtier — thou the curate!
Sister, how shall we endure it?

FLURRIEL

Only spirit-craft can cure it.
        [*Whispers.*]
Dost thou hear?

FERVIAN

Tell me, dear.

FLURRIEL

Sober taciturnity,
Staid religion, pleases thee;
Wagging tongue and wit for me!

[*Taking out a small gold vial.*]

Use then *this*, and thou shalt see
Merry wonders. At its zest,
Each shall have what suits her best;
For, by means of this sly nurture,
A knight shall don a monk's deporture,
And a curate change to courtier.

[*Knocking at the outer door. Flurriel, in hurried whispers, shows Fervian how to smear liquid from the vial upon her left hand. This she does. The knockings grow louder. Exit Flurriel in laughter.*]

FERVIAN

Saints! what din!
Come in — come in!

[*Enter Babblebrook, bowed under a great pack of firewood, strapped to his shoulders.*]

BABBLEBROOK

Art thou the bell which struck that heavenly tone,
That silvery mandate?

FERVIAN

What, good sir?

BABBLEBROOK

" Come in."
It fell upon my heart like wedding bells.

Or like the sweet, premonitory din
That preludes dinner-time.

FERVIAN
           Sir, what impels —

BABBLEBROOK
Bid me not be a sandalled Capuchin
To nurse chilblains, and fast on mackerels
In a monastery; yet such, beauteous maid,
Must be my fate if thou disdain me. Lo!
Fair Sylvia, I kneel!
[*Kneeling, he loses his balance; the load of fire-logs is precipitated, with a crash, upon the hearth; thus prostrate, he addresses her.*]
           I love you.

FERVIAN
      [*Aside.*]
                    Aid
Me now, quick magic!
[*As if to assist him, she extends her left hand; he seizes it.*]

BABBLEBROOK
           Queenly maid, I know
This matchless hand without more introduction.
A subtle influence makes me aware
Thou art the sylvan nymph of my seduction.
Time flies, and wooers flock. To arms! I swear
        [*Kisses her hand.*]
Even by this kiss –

FERVIAN
      [*Aside.*]
    The magic works!

BABBLEBROOK

[*Glowering, starts from her gloomily.*]

                                  Abduction!

[*He stalks away.*]

O woman! — sounding brass and tinkling cymbal!

                                  [*Exit, at back.*]

FERVIAN

O man! poor patch-quilt, stitched by Clotho's thimble!

                                  [*Exit, right.*]

[*Enter Flurriel, dragging Sob after her through the outer door. Running to a chair, she places opposite it another; in these they sit.*]

FLURRIEL

[*As she enters.*]

Come, merry Master Sob, come in! This is
The game. Here, sit, so!

SOB

                    As my rule applies,
I do not play games, Madam Sylvia.

FLURRIEL

                             Oh,
But this one's wise; it treats of cooking. — Eyes
This way! Hands flat!

[*Here Flurriel teaches Sob the hand pantomime, which constitutes the familiar nursery-game of " Pease-porridge hot," wherein Sob manifests the extremity of awkward confusion. Enter Sylvia, who looks on unobserved.*]

SOB

So?

FLURRIEL
[*Nods.*]
                    Good. Now, out! — No, no!
Then up!
                SOB
    But what —?

            FLURRIEL
            Now!
        [*Aside.*]
                    In a wink or two,
The honey's magic on my mouth shall turn
The spirits of my bumble-bee.
[*With increasing rapidity, Flurriel alone, then Flurriel and Sob
    together, repeat the following:*]

            Pease-porridge hot,
            Pease-porridge cold,
            Pease-porridge in the pot
            Nine days old.
            Some like 'em hot,
            Some like 'em cold,
            Some like 'em in the pot
            Nine days old.
[*Breaking into peals of laughter, Flurriel kisses Sob on the lips,
    and, taking both his hands, dances twice round; then,
    pushing him toward the outer door, turns and runs the
    other way; there, seeing Sylvia, she stifles her laughter and
    exit. Sob, at the instant of the kiss, is transformed; in
    the doorway, reeling and hilarious, he bawls out to Sylvia.*]

                SOB
            Some like 'em hot,
            Some like 'em cold,

THE REVERIE

Some like 'em in the pot
Nine days old.
                        We'll do!
'Odd's porridge-pots! we'll do!
            [*Exit.*]

SYLVIA

                Can lovers yearn
For lunacy! — for honey'd lips, that skew
The garb of nature inside out, and sear
Even with the senses' first satiety?
How otherwise is love!

[*Enter, from without, Felix and Somnus; the latter, after pointing out Sylvia to Felix, immediately retires outside. Felix goes swiftly to Sylvia, who is standing in a brown study, and addresses her.*]

FELIX

Sylvia, at last I find you. Sylvia! Mute?
Love, even you? Are you too held from me
Like a white goddess in the unhewn marble
Whom only Fancy sees? Are you, too, walled
Incarcerate within this reverie,
This crystalline, cold castle of conceit?
And through its adamant of moated silence
Is all incursion, all egress, denied?

[SYLVIA]

              True love makes clear
Man's natural aptitudes, lifts them to be
His eternal goads to service.

FELIX

My words! — still mine. I am hung round with them
As with wove, pictured tapestries, through which
My muffled heart cries out in vain. O Sylvia!

SYLVIA
[*Stirring as from a trance.*]
Felix!
[*She holds out her hands to him; he takes them passionately
and kisses them.*]

FELIX
Thank God! I am alone no more.

SYLVIA
I have much needed you. How did you come?

FELIX
I know not how, beloved; but I know
That this is you, and where you are joy is.

SYLVIA
Who brought you here?

FELIX
An old, strange man; his name
He said, is Somnus.

SYLVIA
He!
[*With pitying scrutiny.*]
Poor Felix!

FELIX

        Tears?
O God! I had forgot my errand. You
Must leave this place — and now! Near by, there lurks
A troop of suitors, seeking out your hand:
Two are poor numbskulls, harmless; but the third —
Ah me! — how shall I name him? He is base,
Yet beautiful in quick perceptions. He,
By lancing with his eye the breast of heaven
To drink cold Nature's milk of starlight; by
Probing the hearts of roses for their fragrance;
By chemistry of logic, his black-art;
But, most, by that rare, subtle sense of beauty,
Whose seed, sown in the reason, blooms to a poet, —
He, by these means, dear love, has guessed your secret,
And comes even now, brooding ambitious rape
Of your dominions and your precious self.

SYLVIA

Sandrac, you mean.

FELIX

     You know him, then? Ah, true;
This living dream has steeped my memory
In mist. — Fly from him, Sylvia!

SYLVIA

       Fly? You bid
The baited fawn, when the big hounds bark near,
To fly! — Will she not *plead* to fly?

FELIX

       You mean —

SYLVIA

I mean that you have plighted me to Sandrac
And shackled us with inevitability.
You bid me fly, yet force me still to stay
To tread the mazes of your comedy.

FELIX

How could I guess — Ah! hear, love, my defence!

SYLVIA

The mightiest defence is penitence.
Recall your lofty promise, when you sought
Me first; retrace its fall — your fall; then, will
Its resurrection — which is yours.

FELIX
                    I will!
If only I could wear your fetters now
Even as a red-hot mail of brass, how I
Would smile to do it! Recall how first I sought
And found you? Always! — Dreaming after tasks
In college, on a snowy twilight, when
The bells had ceased — my Plato laid aside —
I pored upon your song young Shakspere sang,
Till "Who is Sylvia?" pealed through all the hush
Miraculous chimes; and there, a sudden genius,
You stood — above your forehead, the first star!

SYLVIA

Your star!

FELIX
          You then, a spirit free as air,
I sunk in clay. You — ardent for my earth,

I — for your heaven. There, rapt in wonder, I
Besought you come and dwell in my world; you,
Besought me how. Do you remember?

SYLVIA
[*Smiling tenderly.*]
                                        Felix!

FELIX
So then I told you of a middle land,
That borders half on Fancy, half on Reason —
A magic bourne where spirits and mortals meet,
Named in the inner world Imagination,
In the outer, called the Stage. There, if you'd come,
I'd give you vesture of fair flesh and blood,
Not such as mortals ache and languish in,
Nor such as saints and goddesses take on
In mural tints and marble; but live speech
That vaults like rapture through immortal veins,
And pours sweet influence in the ears of men.

SYLVIA
'Twas beautiful! And even as Spring gives thanks
To every flower that breathes her to the world,
I blessed each teeming thought of yours, that gave
My yearning heart expression.

FELIX
                          So you did,
And those your blessings fell like fragrant showers.
But there was more. Within that middle land,
I said, we two should meet. I should cut out

My airy likeness from the stuff of fancy
To clothe my own true being.   Thus we'd be
Eternal lovers in our play of time.

                    SYLVIA
Why could it not have been!

                    FELIX
                              Pondering upon,
Your spirit powers, the realm you promised me,
And the homage men would pay me, in the throne
Of strong success, 'twas then that in my brain,
Self-bred, with sudden rupture and sick pang,
Sandrac was born.
                    SYLVIA
          Ah, horrible!

                    FELIX
                              At first,
I thought him beautiful as he seemed wise,
For he was versed in such Socratic art
As made me deem — heaven help me! — that *you*
    loved him;
That he, not I, deserved your sovereign joy,
And therefore, with a mawkish self-deceit,
I inveigled you for him into my play
And plighted you as lovers. — Ah!   but hear me!

                    SYLVIA
                 [*Changing.*]
Good bye!
                    FELIX
          Where are you going?   Sylvia!

SYLVIA
                              Back
Into the play.
          FELIX
          But you are free!

          SYLVIA
                         No, no;
You chose a happy moment, when my part
Was in soliloquy, which for a little
Left me my freedom: Now — ah, now I feel
The irresistible wires compel me.

          FELIX
                         Oh,
That I should make of you a dial-puppet
To obey the petty clockwork of my mind!

          SYLVIA
Farewell, my Felix! Keep your faith. Though I
Be lost — a silvery dove, in your soul's fog-bank,
Still, while you grope and call for me, your mate,
Know that I, too, will seek you as the sunlight.

          FELIX
You shall not need. My will shall be a wind
To rend those mists.
          SYLVIA
[Struggling against the change, which begins to overwhelm her.]
                    Alas! It whirls me on
To utter your irrevocable lines.

FELIX
Say not irrevocable! Sandrac — *he*
Will come!
SYLVIA
   It must be.
[*Oblivious, and transformed in manner,* **she turns to Flurriel,
who enters.**]

FELIX
              Never ! Sylvia!
Dissolved! — dissolved like foam in the black current;
The stream flows on; and I alone on the bank!

[SYLVIA]
              What now, dear?

FLURRIEL
Another wooer, mistress — the Oxford scholar
Is coming up the wood-path.

SYLVIA
             Then you'll please
Me, Flurry, by receiving this new caller.
Nay, cozen him with any coquetries
You will. He'll think you're Sylvia, I dare say.

FLURRIEL
That's it; he must, if he should see me first.
I warn you, then; he'll think you witless.

SYLVIA
                  Mercy!
I hope he will, my dear! I have no thirst
For lovers, or their praises; for, from hearsay,

They are a fickle species. Better burst
With laughter than with love, say I. Adieu!
                [*Exit.*]

                FLURRIEL
Strange! when I saw this wooer through the casement,
It set me all ashiver. I feel blue.
Yet why?
             [*She stands pondering.*]

                FELIX
I'll tell you, Flurriel.

               [FLURRIEL]
      I wonder what his smiling face meant?
The smile was more a scowl than —

                FELIX
         Do not trust him.

             [FLURRIEL]
[*Looking through the casement, gives a startled cry.*]
                      I'll hide too.
          [*Exit.*]

                FELIX
       [*Shouts.*]
                            Flurriel
Flurriel! — So, still doomed to the dumb failure!
When I still swayed these beings with my pen,
And felt them stirring in my ink, like fish,
Nibbling the bait of fancy — ah! when I
Paced my book'd study with a beating heart
And gazed them in the face with my soul's eye,
Then — then, I lorded over them. I saw

Them plain, yes, plainer than I see them now
I made them speak, laugh, scheme — my puppet show,
Fingered them like a god, in short, yet now
The waxworks I devised walk away from me.
By heaven! it shall not be. They're mine; they're mine;
I made them; 'twas my will. — Ah, me! my will! —
Too true — my will! O Sylvia, was that I,
Who bodied him — *him*, gave him clay of thought,
Where, like a hermit-wasp, in his mud nest,
He might secrete and cherish his foul sting,
And then, bid him sting — *you!* No, no, he shall not!
He's mine, I say! He must not, shall not, live!

[*Sandrac, knocking softly, enters. Somnus follows him in.*]

SANDRAC
May I come in?

FELIX
And still he lives, and talks with a dead tongue.

[SANDRAC]
None here? 'Tis quick erasement;
I saw a pretty profile on the pane
A moment since.

[*Felix approaches Sandrac with a look of scorn; Somnus steps calmly between them. Enter Flurriel.*]

Ah, here! — Is this the home
Of Hikrion and his daughters?

FLURRIEL
[*Assuming a dignity.*]
'Tis, sir!

SANDRAC

Then
Send Sylvia here.

FLURRIEL
[*Between fear and amazement.*]
Sir? — Sylvia?

SANDRAC
Bid her come
To meet a stranger.

FLURRIEL
[*Aside, withdrawing slowly.*]
Does he jest, or feign?
Takes he not *me* for Sylvia?

SANDRAC
[*Knitting his brows.*]
Well?
[*Flurriel frightened, curtsies and exit. Sandrac looks round him, smiling.*]
Her room!

FELIX
What will he do? My mind is spinning round.
I have forgot the sequence of this scene.
[*During the rest of the scene, Felix watches all with a tense and painful curiosity.*]

[*Reënter Flurriel, bringing Fervian.*]

FLURRIEL
[*Aside to Fervian.*]
He saw through *me* at once. I tried in vain
To cozen him.

FERVIAN

[*With quiet dignity, to Sandrac.*]

Good-day, sir. I am called
To meet a stranger?

SANDRAC

Yes, a jewel-seeker,
Whose eye can sift green glass from emerald.

FERVIAN

Why, so this maid has told me; you were quicker
To spy her paste out than the amateur.

SANDRAC

Quite so; and still less shall I cry " Eureka! "
Now on beholding you. Where's Sylvia? Her
I sent for.

FERVIAN

Well, sir?

SANDRAC

Tush! I know you two;
I seek your mistress, not her maids.

FLURRIEL

[*Aside to Fervian.*]

He's bent
On finding her. Alas! what shall we do?

FERVIAN

[*Proudly to Sandrac.*]

I know not by what right of high descent,
Or worth, you lord it here. You came to woo,
Methinks, and not to wield the sceptre of
Supremacy.

THE REVERIE

SANDRAC

What matters that to you
Why I came here?

FERVIAN

My life, sir; for I love
My — my —
[*Stops confused.*]

SANDRAC

Your mistress, Sylvia; — say it!

FERVIAN

Yes,
Since by the theft of some bright power above,
You have unlocked her secret, I confess
That we are Sylvia's handmaids. But I adore
My mistress; ere my lips shall syllable
Her secrets, I'll be dumb for evermore.

FLURRIEL

[*Clinching her teeth.*]
Our hearts are locked with ivory chains.

SANDRAC

Well, well!
You will unfasten them if you are wise.
What, never? Why, then, they may need a spell
To ope them, like the Sleeping Beauty's eyes.

FELIX

What's that?

SANDRAC

Whist! Listen!
[*He brings his face close to Flurriel's.*]
Gentle spirit!
[*Whispers to her.*]

FLURRIEL

Fervian! Save
Me, save!

SANDRAC

[*To Fervian.*]

How fares thy fairy princess, she
Who frolics as a maid by day?

FERVIAN

You rave!

SANDRAC

Nay, she to whom, by moonlight minstrelsy,
Thou singest: "Who is Sylvia?" — Dost thou speak?
Art thou not "dumb for evermore?"

FELIX

That I could silence him!

[*Somnus restrains Felix.*]

FERVIAN AND FLURRIEL

[*Kneeling.*]

Great master!

FERVIAN

Pity for Sylvia!

SANDRAC

Nay, though she is weak
And I am strong, such knowledge need not blast her.
I know her secret; therefore by her vow
She needs must wed me; yet I'll haste no faster
To bind her spirit-crown upon my brow
Than is in keeping with a maid's convention
And my own convenience. Till to-night I allow,
When I'll make formal shrift of my intention
Before her Fairy Court. There I have sworn its
Accomplishment.

THE REVERIE

FERVIAN

But —

SANDRAC

If you give detention
To my desires, I'll have you stung with hornets
And smeared with vinegar.

FELIX

O baser than all beasts!

[SANDRAC]

I'll keep my eye on
You both. — When shall we meet?

FERVIAN

When through the torn nets
Of silken eve, bursts the sun's glaring lion,
And shakes his golden mane, with bloodshot eye,
Then blinks and lays him couchant 'neath Orion,
Come forth and meet us in the wood near by.
We'll show you Sylvia.

SANDRAC

[*Smiling, takes up his cloak.*]
I shall be there.

FLURRIEL

[*On Fervian's shoulder, sobbing.*]

And I.

FERVIAN

[*Faintly.*]

And I.

FELIX

[*As Somnus beckons him away — looks back at Sandrac.*]
And I.

[CURTAIN.]

SCENE II: *Twilight; the edge of the wood, with Sylvia's ivy-grown cottage against a golden wing of the sunset. A path leads to the cottage, through a stile in the garden-hedge. Near by, a jet of gleaming water is pouring into a quiet fountain.*
Enter, left, Alberto, playing improvisations on his violin. He wanders back and forth, pausing at times with his ear bent lovingly over his instrument, lost in the rapture of his own strains. He is followed by Pierre, who pays slight attention to the music. In a bustling manner, he seeks to find the right position for his easel, which — after shifting about and scrutinizing the sunset between his hands, and with slanted cheek — he unfolds, and sets up in front of the cottage. Here he sits, looking off right to the setting sun, and commencing a sketch. From the opposite side enter Felix and Somnus. They stop and listen to the touching cadences of Alberto's violin.]

FELIX

Hark! 'Tis the love-sigh of a sad immortal
Breathed to a mortal maiden! — How the sound
Yearns through the solemn wood, and emulates
The silver diapason of a thrush.

[They draw nearer.]

O hark again, and still! His instrument
Is strung with rushes of a naiad's lute,
And modulated with an angel's wand.

SOMNUS

His is the mightiest voice in my dominions.

THE REVERIE

[*Alberto sits at the foot of a tree, seeming to follow a bird's flight with his eyes. Felix approaches him.*

FELIX

Strange boy, I love you dearly; yet I envy,
For you are the bard of that blind eloquence
Which rages in my soul when words fall wingless;
And robed in your melodious imagery,
My longing speaks colossal metaphor.
Oh! is it not stinging, Somnus, that this lad
May, with a subtle finger-touch, unhinge
Heaven's gate, and scatter tumultuous angels over
The world. Yet I, who made him, I, who'd bleed
My soul out to infuse *my* instrument,
My *play* (of which these men are stops and strings)
With thoughts that loom in me divine and vast,
I cannot wake in him one chord — but silence.

SOMNUS

He and his instrument are one, this bow
Is but another member of his body;
This violin his outward heart. But you
Are all at odds and angles, in rank discord,
With a fair instrument unstrung.

FELIX
       'Tis so.
[*Taking up the violin, which Alberto has momentarily laid down.*]
How I could love this carven creature! Tell me,

Sweet viol, where now is all thy rapture flown?
Is it sipp'd up by those pied forest-birds
Thy master's eyes are following? Is it carried
Off in their throats to the cedary faun, thy father,
Who quaffs the eternal sap of wordless song
From his rough bark-vats? Or still does it linger
Here, like remember'd music of the waves
Lodged in the smooth ear of a pink sea-shell?
[*Lays the violin down, and crossing to Pierre, looks over his shoulder while he paints.*]
Gods! how this fellow daubs his thumbs, to cram
His sated palette with sick greens and yellows,
With never a thought of the heaven he means to paint!

SOMNUS

He is industrious. Look, he will give you
A yellow for a yellow, when all's done.
 [*Alberto begins to play again.*]

FELIX

But not a symbol for a symbol. See
Where Twilight, like a sable-cowlèd monk,
By one white taper, plies his solemn task:
With crimson scroll and golden hieroglyph
To emblazon on the sombre nave of night
The annals of the day that has just died.
Let him translate that gorgeous epitaph
Truthfully here, not copy it like Sanskrit;
So only may he hope to fill the souls
Of men with his own immortality.

SOMNUS
You find the heavens, then, full of human meanings?

FELIX
I find a heavenly meaning still in man.

SOMNUS
Nature, for you, has thoughts?

FELIX
                            Far more! For me,
This world's the self-communing mind of Nature,
Who, like Athene, yet unborn of Jove,
Imagines all that is, and earth and heaven
Are but the content of her helm. Even so
The night-domed zenith, crystalline with worlds,
Is the awful arc of her imponderous skull;
The roseate east and west her pulsing temples,
Flushing her thoughts in sunsets and in mornings;
The coruscating stars and meteors
Are flashes of her cerebration, struck —
Like sparks that crackle through the cable's coil —
From magic fluid. Thus earth, air and all
Convolving forms of cloud and whirling rain
And scattered sunlight are the neural stuff
Of Infinite Reverie, and we ourselves,
That burrow in the beehive of God's brain,
We men, — are but imaginations, thoughts
That crawl, or fly, in Nature's mind; and some
Are true, and others are but fancies.

SOMNUS

                So;
What, then, is *he?* — a fancy?
[*Enter Sandrac, reading a book. Being dusk, he holds the print close to his eyes.*]

FELIX

[*Clutching Somnus' robe and turning away.*]
                God have pity!
[*Exeunt.*]

SANDRAC

[*Looking up from his book, listens to Alberto.*]
This boy's a master; he has ecstasy.
[*Alberto, at Sandrac's approach, in the midst of a note of infinite longing, throws away his violin, flings himself on the ground, and sobs hysterically.*]

ALBERTO

                O,
Take her away!   Take her away!
[*Pierre stops painting, looks over his shoulder at Alberto, but seeing Sandrac approach him, resumes his work. Sandrac stands over Alberto.*]

SANDRAC

                Here, here,
Boy, do not cry.

ALBERTO

[*Sobbing to himself.*]
Ah, dio, dio, dio!

SANDRAC
Come, would you make this violet bed your bier?

ALBERTO
I hate her!
> [*Taking up the violin.*]
— Boy!

ALBERTO
[*Leaps to his feet, and snatching his violin from Sandrac's hands, holds it tight to his breast.*]
Let go! What man are you?

SANDRAC
One who may teach you something.

ALBERTO
[*Imperiously.*]
Leave me; leave.

SANDRAC
Not till I tell you why your love's untrue.

ALBERTO
She's not; she's not!
> [*Kisses his violin.*]

SANDRAC
Then, why, pray, do you grieve?

ALBERTO
You're not my priest; farewell!
> [*Turns away.*]

SANDRAC

                Stay, lad; I like
Your manners, and I know your mind. You're sad
Because your violin here will not strike
A chord as sweet as your soul does. You're mad
To dream it can.

ALBERTO

           I am not mad; you lie!

SANDRAC

           [*Harshly.*]
Then fiddle on, and fail until you die.

[*Alberto, with heaving breast, lifts his violin to his chin, and commences playing, at first with moving inspiration, but then with sudden fall into a cheerless commonplace. He stops, utterly disheartened.*]

ALBERTO

She's false; but oh, I loved her! Listen, sir;
This thing that you call " it " — this wood — I named
Bella, and as a sweetheart, worshipped her
Near half my life.

SANDRAC

            Still dreaming to be famed
Through her, still failing. Yes, I know. I too
Am but a convalescent fool even now.

ALBERTO

Famed? No, I didn't think of that. — To imbue
Her heart with my own joy, that was my vow;
And now, 'tis broken. Ah, *I* am the traitor!

SANDRAC

No, my young friend, you're puzzled; half right, but
Half wrong. You thought, forsooth, since you could mate a
Live spirit of Art to this dry, mummied gut,
Their offspring would be Joy; whereas, 'tis Yearning.
But I will cure you with a little learning.

ALBERTO

[*Throws himself on a bank, plucking up violets and anemones, which he strews about.*]

I wish I were well shovelled in the earth
That wild flowers then might spring from me!

SANDRAC

                                            That would
Be planting woe for others to pluck mirth.
Nay, boy, there's no good in another's good,
Unless it be invested for our own.

ALBERTO

Then give me no more of your good advice.
        [*Turns away, still lying on the bank.*]

SANDRAC

Well answered, by Minerva! with a tone
That's unambiguous. Your heart is thrice
More keen-eyed than your brain. Therefore I will
Advise you something further for your profit: —
        [*Points to Hikrion's cottage.*]
There dwells an heiress. By your master skill
In art, you'd win her fortune. Come! think of it,
And let this cast-off love
        [*Indicating the violin.*]

go catch a new.
Sylvia's her name.

PIERRE
[*Turning about.*]
That might be hard to do.

SANDRAC
[*To Pierre.*]
Ah, friend, how's that?

PIERRE
Perchance he comes too late.

SANDRAC
So, so? — Ah, that's because *you* seek her hand,
Perhaps?

PIERRE
Why, now you've hit it.

SANDRAC
Here's a state
Of woe for all the rest o' the world. — Good! and
Who, friend, may you be?

PIERRE
[*Still painting.*]
Pierre, the Painter.

SANDRAC
He
Who has not heard of Raphael, be chid;
But he who knows not Pierre, the Painter, be
Damned ignoramus. — What, sir! have you hid
Your fame in this far forest?

PIERRE
                A short space
Till I shall take this Sylvia home.

SANDRAC
                        To Paris?

PIERRE
Of course; where else? That is the only place.

SANDRAC
[*Signifying with a gesture his desire to look at the painting.*]
May I — ?

PIERRE
[*Stopping his work and showing the picture with condescension.*]
           Yes, yes, look; to all Dicks and Harrys
I do not show my works; but you appear
To have some eye and temperament; look here!
    [*Pierre holds up the painting. Sandrac looks at it long.*]

SANDRAC
Striking!

PIERRE
      N'est ce pas? What think you of me?

SANDRAC
                                   Eh?
I think that if some kind friend tweaked your nose
You'd deem he stroked you on the cheek, to say
You are the first of fellows. But God knows,
There's been enough of this. If I may advise,
To-morrow Sylvia here will hold a test
Of all her suitors, she herself the prize
Of him who her three questions answers best —

Best meaning rightly. Sirs, to lovers, hints
Are good as hatchets to build houses. So
Good night!

PIERRE
[*Who has gathered up his things in hot fury.*]
Which path go you, pray, Monsieur Squints!

SANDRAC
This way.

PIERRE
[*Taking the opposite direction.*]
Then I go this.
[*Exit, fuming.*]

SANDRAC
[*Calls after him.*]
To Sylvia, ho!

[*He laughs a hard, keen laugh. Alberto, who has laid his violin on Sylvia's door-sill, is just leaving it in despair. Sandrac detains him.*]

Stay! — Where now, boy?

ALBERTO
[*Tearing himself away.*]
I'll come alone to-morrow.
[*Exit.*]

SANDRAC
Meantime to-night my joy shall be their sorrow.
But now to find my lady's handmaids.

[*He goes to the edge of the wood, peering off, and slowly exit.*]

[*Enter Felix and Somnus.*]

FELIX

The dusk grows darker now and darkness brighter,
For slowly now the soft, round moon grows keen.

SOMNUS

The appointed time is almost here.

FELIX

                       O Night,
Thou Afric skull for Attic contemplation,
How many worlds the teeming mind of man
Has, like a sun, given off to sate your chaos,
And never regathered with centripetal hand!
Where shall he track their orbits yon, their systems, —
He that would weave a garland of the stars
And wear it lightly like a shepherd's crown?
Thicker than sparks that glut the smithy's chimney
Thou hast devoured them. I wonder, Night,
Are those eternal torches there aloft
Borne by the pallid hands of mortal thinkers
Searching the vaults of heaven for their lost dreams?
If so, no marvel that their name is legion.

SOMNUS

Is not this place your rendezvous?

FELIX

                       What then?
Now is the autumn season of the day

The sunset hour of sere musings. Let
Me dream.

SOMNUS

And set your dreams in action — when?
[*Exeunt.*]

[*After a brief pause, enter, left, Fervian and Flurriel. From the right, reënters Sandrac.*]

SANDRAC
       Met
At last! You're late come. Is not this the hour
When Sylvia holds her fairy court?

FERVIAN
       Not yet,
For yet but three lamps hang in Twilight's tower,
And we must wait until Night signals nine,
One for each handmaid of the perfect moon
That reigns in heaven for Sylvia.

SANDRAC
       When those shine —
What then?

FERVIAN
     When breaks the ninth star, thou shalt soon
Behold the rest. Meantime, and during all
Of awe thou mayst behold, secrete thee near
Behind this holly-bush, through whose scant wall,
Thou mayst discover all unseen.

SANDRAC
       And hear
The song of Sylvia?

FERVIAN
Yes.

SANDRAC
              The enchanted key
Of music that unlocks her destiny!
Here on this parchment I will write it down
To-night; then, at to-morrow's trial, read
It forth to Sylvia and claim her crown.

FLURRIEL
        [*To Fervian.*]
What have we done?

FERVIAN
          A tyrant's hateful deed,
Not ours!
    [*To Sandrac.*]
        Stay, sir; it will be futile there
On parchment to inscribe her song, unless
You know its inmost meaning. Therefore, pray,
Inscribe it not.

SANDRAC
         And so fail of my guess
To-morrow? — Fools, had I no other way
To riddle out your mistress' heart, think ye
I'd walk so proud a pace, and ye so quailing?
This method is succinct and pleases me —
To net her with her song. But as for failing
In the end, why, gawks! my power has myriad ways:
Fetch me yon glow-worm.

[*Flurriel, stooping, picks up a faint phosphorescent light and gives it to Sandrac.*]

FLURRIEL
Here.

[*Sandrac holds it on his palm, and blows it; immediately it leaps into a white, electric flame, which glorifies the wood with an intense brilliance, revealing in the distance the approaching figures of Felix and Somnus; then relapsing to its former dimness in the moonlight. Fervian and Flurriel recoil and hide their faces in fear.*]

SANDRAC
So can I blaze
The palest spark of beauty for my ends,
Till it shall fathom time with fulguration
And weave a nimbus for the world. — Night wends;
Enough; begone!

FERVIAN
But, master —

SANDRAC
Know your station.
Begone!

FERVIAN
We must.

[*They pass into the house.*]

SANDRAC
Yonder's the sixth star. I'll
Couch me and wait.

[*He retires behind the holly-bush, where he is dimly seen, poring over a book by the light of the glow-worm, which flames duskily in the hollow of a stump. Reënter Felix and Somnus.*]

FELIX
Inexorable jailer! Show her mercy!
Open some door of liberation.

SOMNUS
     Only
He sets her free, whose strong, expanded spirit
Can wrench my bars and win her.

FELIX
      Pitiless,
Relentless ghost! You know I cannot do it,
And so you plague me.

SOMNUS
   Nay, I know it not.

FELIX
Come, then; you know we found a subterfuge
Before to speak with her.

SOMNUS
    Well?

FELIX
      If I find
Another, will you guide me? — Answer!

SOMNUS
       Yes;
If in this wall of mortised words and will
Which you have builded, I can prod some flaw,
Or secret breach, to slip you through to her,
I'll do so.

FELIX

    I can show you one. For I
Remember, in this very act and scene
Where now we tread, I left a void of thought,
Thinking to fill it up, in the manuscript,
When I should grow more wise. It is the place
Where Sylvia's handmaids, having gone their ways
On mortal errands, leave her quite alone,
Dreading the approach of Sandrac. There the scene
Is left unsolved — chaotic. Through that gap,
Then, let me pass to speak with her.

SOMNUS

          So be it.
Yet do not think that such a subterfuge
Shall set her free. What has been willed is willed
Until it be revok'd. Thou shalt be duped,
And her once more your creatures shall enthrall.

FELIX

Yet she shall hear — shall speak to me once more?

SOMNUS

She shall.

FELIX

    God help me, then: I'm willing.

SOMNUS

          Look!

SANDRAC
[*Starting up.*]
  The ninth star shines.

THE REVERIE

[*The cottage of Sylvia changes to an ample palace, of which the trees form pillars, supporting a roof of glowing vaults, which increase in radiance and thicker-thronging stars as the scene advances. Sylvia, as a spirit, is discovered seated upon a single throne, surrounded by her nine handmaidens, each of whom is leader of a throng of lesser spirits; these, as the scene opens, are grouped about the throne, singing. While they sing, Sandrac, crouching again by the stump, listens and writes on his parchment.*]

THE SPIRITS

Who is Sylvia? What is she
  That all her swains commend her?
Holy, fair and wise is she;
The heaven such grace did lend her
  That admirèd she might be.

Is she kind as she is fair,
  For beauty lives with kindness.
To her eyes love doth repair
To help him of his blindness,
  And being helped inhabits there.

SYLVIA

[*Standing, bids them, by a gesture, cease their song.*]

Spirits of Fancy, Pan's immortal Elves,
I thank you. Yet, since praises are but pride
Unless they sing deeds sweeter than themselves,
We will to our to-night's affairs, nor bide
One instant of obsequious court. Come, then!
And from our hands take missions unto men.

[*They come to her. She whispers. They depart. Sandrac, who has been alert, watching all, now — dropping his parchment — sinks into a stupor.*]

FELIX

Quick, Somnus! 'Tis the instant. All is still.
This is the gap I left in the scene. Release me!

SOMNUS

Does Sandrac speak no more?

FELIX

                      I think, no more:
No more that I remember. — Lead me to her!
See, she awakes.

SOMNUS

Wait here.

SYLVIA

[*Reaching her arms upward in joy.*]
                      Ah, free again!

SOMNUS

[*Approaching Sylvia.*]
Immortal Maid, and Empress of Delight,
Out of the mist-keep of mortality
I come to beg my sovereign a boon.

SYLVIA

Speak, Somnus: what dark tale of mortal madness,
Or sad irresolution, do you bring
From out your dungeon?

SOMNUS

              I bring no story,
But one who brings a story.

SYLVIA

              What, a mortal?
Lives there indeed on earth a modern Samson,
That can disjoint the impalpable pillars of
His prison house, and through his blindness' wreck
See heaven?

SOMNUS

           If such there be, I bring him not.
This one has sought a subterfuge.   His name
Is Felix.

SYLVIA

    O, where is he?

[*Somnus beckons, Felix springs passionately from his covert.*]

FELIX

        Here, love!

[*Somnus withdraws and stands over Sandrac.*]

SYLVIA

                  Welcome!

FELIX

Am I, then, welcome still, though still my love
Is impotent?

SYLVIA

       Can love be impotent?
Why, I should be a futile, heart-broke thing
Without your warm, live, human heart to love me.

FELIX

[*Embracing her.*]

Though it be weak, it beats an enduring song
Like a goldsmith in bright silver. Can you hear it?

SYLVIA

How true it rings!

FELIX

That is because it hammers
Your name, love. Listen: *Sylvia — Sylvia — Sylvia —*
'Tis forging an inner shrine to worship you.

SYLVIA

My subtle poet!

FELIX

No, your steadfast lover.
Too oft from you my probing mind is errant —
Never my heart! That's poised, a centred pole,
Round which my vague-eyed, sheering fancies whirl
Like Cassiopeia and the Pleiades
Around the north. O Sylvia, bear with me
Though still the poet speaks! For I have come
To beg this night our boon of union: not
Such meeting as of mortal earth with earth,
But blending of that earth with mystery,
As when, in March, from out the starved sod, springs
Beauty!

SYLVIA

Why do you ask this? Do you crave
Me, or my crown? Ah, dear, forgive the doubt!

THE REVERIE

I would make sure. — Alas! there has been need
Ere now.

FELIX
There has been need, but now no more,
I swear!

SYLVIA
Consider: he who wins my crown
Shall earn an immortality of praise,
Become an epithet in the ear of time,
And stun the coming ages with his name.
Are none of these your motives?

FELIX
None, I swear!
SYLVIA
By what sufficient goddess do you swear?

FELIX
[*Looking upward.*]

There! In that open locket of white pearl
Which Cynthia wears, a night-charm, on her breast —
There shines the virgin-mistress of my vows,
Whose image of ideality men name
The Lady in the Moon. Look, Sylvia!
The lineaments of that shadow luminous
Are yours. Long ere the first, sad dreamer kneeled,
Her smile bent o'er the clouds of earth, benign —
A blessing and a lure to aspiration.
Hers is that brow which he of Melos Isle
Wrought in long-buried marble; gazing on her,
Young Raphael learned to mure adoring ardor

In *The Transfiguration*. Hers and yours
And Beauty's are one profile. — Therefore, there
By your perennial portrait in the heaven,
Your deathless image in Night's darkling eye —
By her — the Lady in the Moon — I swear.

[*Smiling wistfully, Sylvia holds out her arms toward Felix. Simultaneously Sandrac (at a touch from Somnus), starting from his stupor, leaps to his feet.*]

SANDRAC

Am I, then, dreaming? What! She calls me. Ah!
She welcomes me to her arms now —

FELIX

[*Starting forward cries aloud simultaneously with Sandrac.*]

Sylvia!
Sylvia!

[*The palace and Sylvia disappear in instant darkness. Groping, the three figures draw together.*]

SOMNUS

[*To Felix.*]

You had forgot; but I remembered.

FELIX

[*Bitterly, at Sandrac's ear.*]

Fool!

[CURTAIN.]

ACT III

ACT III

Scene: Exterior of Sylvia's cottage; the same scene as the opening of Act II, Scene II. Noon.

Near the fountain, Hikrion is seated; on one of his great knees, the slender figure of Alberto is perched, scanning his shrewd face.

HIKRION
[*Chanting deeply.*]
In the bottom, in the bottom, of a pond a nix was wed!

ALBERTO
Where, did you say?

HIKRION
Ah, who was her bridegroom there?
A drownèd man, a drownèd man!

ALBERTO
Not dead!

HIKRION
[*Sepulchrally.*]
Who gave her away? gave her away?

ALBERTO
Don't stare
So, dad!

HIKRION
[*Smiling merrily.*]
A pretty pout; her eyes were blue
And 'r fins were frill'd.

[*Darkly.*]

But tell! who was best man!
The silvery, slippery water-snake: he knew
The service.

ALBERTO

[*Struggling to get off Hikrion's knee, is held tight by him.*]

Let me go!

HIKRION

Nay, tell if ye can!
Who was the choir! — I know! The mud-frogs; they
Were choir, were choir —

[*Stentorianly.*]

for the drownéd, drownéd man.

ALBERTO

Quick! Let me go.

HIKRION

What, are ye uneasy, eh?
How old are ye, lad!

ALBERTO

I am past seventeen;
I'm not a youngster to be knee-danced.

HIKRION

[*Pushing him off and rising.*]

Nay,
Then, off with ye, fair gentleman; ye're clean
Too growed up for a lad like me.

ALBERTO

[*Returning to Hikrion and hugging him.*]

No, no.
I love to listen. — Please!

THE REVERIE

HIKRION

[*Turning away roughly.*]

                                  Nay, get along.
Ye're like the rest o' them that come to woo
My daughter: so ingenious ye go wrong
When a simple hand would wind ye.

ALBERTO

[*Burying his face in his arms against a tree.*]

                                  Fool! Fool! I'll
Go drown and wed the nix.

HIKRION

[*Returning with a kind smile.*]

                                  Pho! boy, a song
Will cheer ye. I was joking.

ALBERTO

[*Looking up.*]

                            Honest?

HIKRION

[*Puts his arm over Alberto's shoulder.*]

                                      Smile,
That's it. Come here and sun ye!

[*They sit on the stile together.*]

                                  Now we'll be
Such like o' lovers as two greenish collies
That wag their tails at each other, when they see
One t'other's ears perk up. Age puts off 's follies
O' puppyhood, folks say; yet the old dog romps

Wi' the young un in the sunshine. Be as jolly as
Nature, says I!

ALBERTO

       Yes, Papa Hikrion, dumps

Are devils!

HIKRION

       Play this pipe, then — it will ease
Ye. Do ye mind the old song " Huswif's Joy "?

ALBERTO

I know it.

HIKRION

      Pipe, then.

[*Alberto pipes and Hikrion sings to his piping.*]

    Three gray housewives plied their stitches
    For to make a goodman a pair of breeches
        And the jerkin of 'em!
        And the jerkin of 'em!
    But when he put 'em on,
    The goodman he was gone,
        Such was the workin' of 'em.
        Lack-a-day!
          Cried the three,
        Which is they?
        Which is he?
    Which is the goodman? Which is?

[*Enter Sob and Babblebrook in the background. They have exchanged their outer garments, Sob assuming a plump swagger in his courtier's dress; Babblebrook in the curate's gown, gravely reading a book of Psalms.*]

ALBERTO

Look! Why, what are these
That come this way?

SOB

[*At the top of his voice.*]

Woodman, woodman, ahoy!

HIKRION

These are a kind o' fowl called golden geese
That quawk in the wood o' mornings. Ay, but what!
They've moulted and changed feathers.

SOB

Woodman!

BABBLEBROOK

[*Glancing up from his book.*]

Peace,
Brother, you mar devotion.

SOB

What of that?
Odds clapper bones and skulls! That peasant rogue
Shall answer me.

[*To Hikrion.*]

You, fellow; look to your hat;
We're gentry.

HIKRION

Be ye?

SOB

Yea, and I'm in vogue
Now, rascal. I will bear no more of your water-
Pails: nor your wood packs; nay, nor heed your brogue
Neither. I'll soon relieve you of your daughter —
Your foster-child. — She kissed me yesterday.
In short, I am approved. Hut — tut!

HIKRION

          I'd ought ter
Be proud o' such a son-in-law, and say,
I really are. There wa'n't another like
Him in the ark, that's certing.

SOB

[*Tugging at his sword.*]

         Sirrah! — Nay,
Thou art the epitome of naught. To strike
Thee, were to eliminate a cipher. Loon,
Tell me, what hour will Sylvia, belike,
Make trial of her suitors?

HIKRION

      Here at noon.

SOB

[*Taking out his purse.*]

Draw near, Chawbacon: this is for your pains.

[*Hands a coin.*]

HIKRION

[*Takes it.*]

A ha'penny! Lor! Sir, you rob your purse!
Yet sith you are so princely, for this gains

[*Holding up the coin.*]

I'll swap ye a pig.

SOB

   A pig!

HIKRION

      Come; that aren't worse
For you; a pig for ha'penny.

THE REVERIE

SOB
Fool!

HIKRION
Got
One here I'll sell ye cheap, eh, laddie?
[*Whispers to Alberto.*]

SOB
Curse
These dolts!

HIKRION
[*Jumping down from the stile, mounts Alberto on his back and shoulders.*]
Up, boy! pig-back. He must be bought,
My masters.
[*Runs after Sob and Babblebrook, who begin to retire, scared.*]

BABBLEBROOK
[*Closing his book.*]
Gracious!

SOB
Stand off!

HIKRION
Buy a pig?

ALBERTO
Gee, Dobbin!

SOB
Base clown — knave — what means this?

HIKRION
Naught;
The epitome of naught: a nursery jig
For babes. Buy a pig? Buy a pig? Buy a pig?

ALBERTO

Gee up! — Whoa, Dobbin! Hah-gee!

[*Hikrion, carrying Alberto on his shoulders, pursues Sob and Babblebrook between the trees, and charges them off the scene. Exeunt omnes. Enter Felix, laughing bitterly; with him Somnus.*]

FELIX

This discourse is the odorous extract of absurdity.

SOMNUS

Whose?

FELIX

Why, ours. What does it come to but star-gazing and ditch-stumbling. But look at this fellow Sandrac; he's no god-gossip. He walks off in my shoes, whistling, while barefoot I stand mooning.

SOMNUS

Ay, so he does.

FELIX

"Ay, so he does!" Old dotard! Yours is the fault of this. You follow me always with your sad assentings, your *so-so's*, and your *too-true's*, or else your crooked question-marks that set me off in labyrinthian descants. What are you, anyway? And why do you dog and nag me, as if I were poor Tom, the cat, that slinks in the dark?

SOMNUS

You know that I am Somnus, the keeper of this wood.

FELIX

Why, yes — my valet-confidant in this drama that's acting. By God! I would you'd let *me* act.

SOMNUS

Do I prevent you?

FELIX

Do you not? You keep me for a soliloquizing magpie.

SOMNUS

I keep you no longer than you will.

FELIX

But I am weary of muttering these asides to you; of playing a most despicable, croaking chorus of one. For look! If this were indeed a theatre, whose boards I tread, — as God knows what it is that's going on here, — why, what a ludicrous guy would I be for a good-natured spectator! Am I the villain? Bah! My blood's too chalk-and-water. Am I the hero? Do I look it? A cuss that skulks and miawls about the side scenes! — Ha! What am I written down as, in the Dramatis Personæ? — Nothing. And what, then, am I? Why, I'm the author: an interruptive, prative, stuttering coxcomb, that puts a make-up on, and issues from the wings to straddle the footlights, neither in nor out of the audience: a walking margin, a superfluous compendium, an insufferable cicerone, that stands like a biograph lecturer, with a long pole, and cries you: "Ladies and Gentlemen, mark this moving figure; this is Babblebrook, this is Sandrac.

I pray you pardon me; I cannot show you that picture again, for the fellow who works the machine is out of hearing." Ahaha! If this indeed were a drama, I say, there's a hero for you!

SOMNUS

It seems you have left *me* out.

FELIX

Oh no; you are the prompter, popped out of his box, in a wig and long-cloak. You kill two birds: first, you're the latest novelty in Hamlet's ghost, which, secondly, gives you the invisible prerogative of whispering the players their lines. Oh! we're a pair of us; we should win an encore from the gods.

SOMNUS

Why, as you say, if this same wood were only a patch of canvas, and we things up for show; *if* we, who act our parts in life, were indeed the made-up semblances we seem to be; *if* the world itself were but a stage, and the stage itself were *all* mere mockery, — yes, then, we should appear such as you say. But all this is *not* so. It seems so to your laughter.

FELIX

And is not laughter the subtlest of our critics?

SOMNUS

Perhaps. All laughter comes from seeing things awry. Who know this, they laugh well; who know it not, and deem they laugh at truth itself — they laugh in hell.

FELIX

Ah, Somnus! you who can teach so thorough the *theory* of human harmony, why cannot you set my flatted mind in tune?

SOMNUS

Why, if you catch my argument, apply it.

FELIX

Apply it? No, no, I *must* laugh, to scratch the itching pox of grief within me.

SOMNUS

Of hate, you mean.

FELIX

Well, hate! What else? I hate him. Should I not? After sick climbing, when I was touching heaven, Sylvia smiling on me, then with a word, a breath, he wraps me in a cloud, and by the heels drags me down, down, to the devil again. Yes, by God's light, I hate him! — deathly, I hate him.

SOMNUS

Will you hate your own offspring?

FELIX

What! Did he not dissipate hope, joy, faith, all, even in my very arms? and has left me now — even as you see me here — a hollow fool of satire? And why not? when Ideality is such a god that, like an urchin's snowman, it melts even in the embraces of its worshipper.

    Ideality! I'd rather carry hods
    For hire, than be a fellow of the gods.
  Ah! But this shall not last. — Come, Somnus.
We will shake this off.

SOMNUS

You must do that.
        [*Exeunt both.*]

[*Enter, from the cottage, Sylvia, dressed in a white sunbonnet, and the costume of a peasant girl. She brings an old-fashioned churn and sets it down near the door.*]

SYLVIA

        In this milk-maid's rig,
I might escape the De'il himself, if he
Came wooing princesses. So farewell terror
Of Sandrac, and his dark conspiracy
To win my hand —What say *you*, pretty mirror?
    [*Bending over the fountain.*]
You make a pretty answer: — jeopardy
To Polly Pinkcheeks' lovers! — Sylvia! bestir, or
Polly will steal thy suitors. — Polly, Polly,
Run fetch thy churning cream, lest thou be chid
By Lady Sylvia. Heigh! sing trolly-lolly
Lo! Heigh! sing trolly-lolly-lee!
    [*Exit into the cottage. Enter Sob and Babblebrook.*]

SOB

                She did
But jest, for she's a runnel of bright wit,
That's ever plashing over.

BABBLEBROOK

                Nay, she's hid
In a sober coif of sadness. She'd permit
No jest to pass her lips.

SOB

              Tut! She is ever
Tripping it like Terpsychore in a fit,
And warbling like an orange-girl.

BABBLEBROOK

                Deliver
Us, heaven! Why, man, her step of pensive grace,
That marches like a still and stately river,
Is set in rhythm to a psalm-tune's pace —
An anapest of motion.

SOB

           "Pease-porridge hot!"
A pensive hymn indeed! I pray you, trace
"Pease-porridge" in the Psalmody.

BABBLEBROOK

              God wot
'Tis there, if Sylvia sung it.

[*Reënter Sylvia with a pail of cream, which she pours into the churn; after which she sits down and begins busily to ply the wooden vertical handle, humming to herself and glancing at the two wooers.*]

SOB

            All thou hast said
Gives proof thou hast not even met her.

K

BABBLEBROOK
                                      Pin
Some arbiter to such a proof.

SOB
            This maid!
[Peeping under Sylvia's bonnet.]
Odds saints and relics! Girl, chuck up thy chin.

SYLVIA
    Too busy;
    Ask the missy;
    Says she, says she.
[Goes on churning and humming.]

SOB
Wench, thou wert by, a-yesterday, when I made
Advances to thy mistress — Wench! wilt stop
A minute? Thou canst bear me witness to
Thy mistress' gay behavior.

SYLVIA
    Bear not false witness
    For master or mistress.
      Hey, bonny Johnny!
        [Churns.]

SOB
      Wench!

SYLVIA
My name's Polly. —
O lassie, be jolly
For your laddie's twenty-four,
And if he's too old, there's plenty more.

THE REVERIE

SOB
Pray drop
Thy stick a moment, Polly.

BABBLEBROOK
Tell us true,
Thou foolish girl, has not thy gentle lady
Sylvia a sober, taciturn, dull hue
Of mind?   Does she not chide thee as unsteady
For singing such crude snatches?

SYLVIA
Nay, she's fond o' butter
As a milk-maid ought 'er.
[*Churns.*]

SOB
But, thou sphinx,
Sylvia's no milkmaid.

SYLVIA
O, ay, fond gentlemen;
To prove: —
She is a milk-white maiden,
My love, my love.

SOB
[*To Babblebrook.*]
Well, sir, I am ready
To uphold it with my sword, that this same minx
Was standing by when Sylvia kissed me; yea,
She smiled when Sylvia smiled; I know the pinks
O' her cheeks, there, underneath her bonnet.

BABBLEBROOK
                                          Nay,
Then she will tell us so. — Good Polly —

SYLVIA
Well, kind Sir,
What of her?
    Churn, churn,
    Youth will yearn.
Johnny said he'd love me ay;
But his love was thin as whey,
When I whipped his words away.
    Churn, churn,
    Live and learn.

BABBLEBROOK
                                          Fie
Upon these females! Take 'em at the core,
They're all alike — a lovesick galaxy.
Sylvia's the only sensible exception
In the sex.

SOB
    Odds crucifixes! Let's not ply
This hussy with more questions. 'Twere direption
Of time. We shall return at noon. Farewell!

SYLVIA
Fare thee well, my true love,
My blue love.
    [*Still churns.*]

BABBLEBROOK
    [*Opening his book.*]
What psalm did I leave off at?

THE REVERIE

SOB
[*With his hands over his ears.*]
Damn!
[*Exeunt Sob and Babblebrook. Sylvia leaps up, laughing.*]

SYLVIA
Deception,
Thy name is — Polly! Pretty Polly, well
Done! Thou shalt have a cracker and cookie
If thou canst play the parrot with such skill
To Milord Sandrac, for I've been told, look'ee,
That he has such an eye as the eagle master
Who spies, in his bench, a bad boy that's played hookie.
[*Suddenly stands on tiptoe and peers.*]
Hist! " Still pond, no fair moving! " Poetaster,
I spy you.
[*She runs again to the churn, plies the wooden handle, and hums.
Enter Sandrac.*]

Churn, churn,
Hearts will burn:
Every Tommy takes his turn.

SANDRAC
What! — a lass?

SYLVIA
Ye may cry alas!
Indeed, poor bonny lass!

SANDRAC
[*To himself.*]
She, as I live!
A cap to hoodwink me! I'll make believe.

[*To Sylvia.*]
So bonny face? Why alas?

      SYLVIA
        'Tis such a pass!
There's no lad to be had.

      SANDRAC
        What will you give
For a lad full grown?

      SYLVIA
        I'll give him tit for tat:
A Roland for an Oliver.

      SANDRAC
[*Stooping over quickly and trying to kiss her.*]
        Then this is
Roland.
 [*Sylvia, striking his cheek, escapes with a laugh.*]

      SYLVIA
And that's his brother, Oliver!
You counterfeit! — *Hearts* are true coin for kisses.

      SANDRAC
      [*Bowing.*]
You've said it prettily.

      SYLVIA
      [*To herself.*]
       Dear Jupiter!
Teach me the mother-tongue of milkmaids.
     [*To Sandrac.*]
          O, sir!
You're most prodigious kind. But I prefer

To hear *you*. You talk prettier 'n our green-grocer,
And he was born in Banbury. I learned
My gentry-talk from him; though you'd suppose a
Plain wench like me, perhaps, had sat and churned
Her wits away. But you, by your fine gown,
Sir, I suppose you are a scholar! — Earned
Much by it? Is 't a good trade?

SANDRAC

Oh! in town,
It is accounted good for threadbare coats,
Lean looks, and penny loaves, and 'tis, I'll own,
A sterile patch for fools to sow wild oats;
Yet for a scholar with an artist's eye
Learning's a pleasant trade. For with the same
He grinds a golden meal called Poesie,
Which then he barters out for fame, and fame
Hoards interest in praise; and so we ply
A paying trade.

SYLVIA

Do you, sir, call a poet,
One who lends genius out for fame.

SANDRAC

I state
Plain business: he who sows a field may mow it;
Who buys is wise to sell at higher rate.

SYLVIA

Your bard's a broker in the Muses' mart;
But *mine*, — a will, whose pregnant powers create
Another Eden in the void of Art,
Where to his creatures he's responsible
That they shall side on God's, not Satan's part.

SANDRAC

What lyric eloquence!

SYLVIA

Me miserable!
I have forgot myself again.
      [*To Sandrac.*]
            'Tis time
I took the butter in. My speech — I'll tell
You, sir, my knack of speech; I learnt it all —
From Sylvia: know her, maybe? — She is — well —
She, sir, 's my mistress! — talks like that — things tall
In sentiment; — and so, of course, we learn —
We maids — from her.

SANDRAC

Ah!

SYLVIA

Sir?
    [*Going to the cottage door.*]
                  Was that a call?
Sir, Sylvia wants me in the house. My churn!
    [*She hurries in, carrying the churn.*]

SANDRAC

Allow me, pray, to help; accept of my —
        [*Exit Sylvia.*]
By Venus! never did my pulse so burn
For starry prizes of astrology,
Nor for the fool's gold-stone, whose secret glitters
In clay, as for this Sylvia. But I

Must drink, one endless instant more, the bitters
Of balked desire.

> [*A pipe plays outside.*]

    What's there? The suitors?

> [*Looks at the sun-dial.*]

              Noon;
Nay, lacks a hair yet. Love and I be sitters
I' the sun till then.

> [*He sits on the edge of the sun-dial and waits. Outside is heard the sound of a pipe and voices, singing.*]

THE VOICES

A lad he longed for a lass:
 Sing wooing and warm weather!
When flocks roamed drowsy on the grass,
 And kine in the tinkly heather.
  " Thou bonny thing,
  Why dost thou wring
 Thy hands in sad beshrewing? "
  Sing wooing!
Sing wooing and warm weather.

A lass she longed for a lad:
 Sing wooing and warm weather!
When first the hill-rose might be had
 And lovers come together.
  " When skies be blue
  And sweethearts few,
 What should a lass be doing? "
  Sing wooing!
Sing wooing and warm weather!

[*The singers enter. First comes Hikrion, with his arm about the shoulder of Alberto, who plays the pipe; then follow, in grouped pairs, Babblebrook and Fervian, Sob and Flurriel, Pierre and Fresca.*]

    Love ripens the longest day;
     Sing wooing and warm weather!
    For pining heart will have his pay,
     And climbing lark his feather.
     " Ere snow shall blow,
      My true love, O!
    There shall be rice a-strewing,"
     Sing wooing!
    Sing wooing and warm weather!

      HIKRION
     A bonny tune;
Well piped, lad! What's the time? — Come, Master Clerk,
I'll thank ye to take your shadow off the dial.
The crow should perch o' nights.

      SANDRAC
     [*Moving aside.*]
        I pray you, mark:
'Tis noon precise.
      HIKRION
     Time, lasses, time for the trial!
Now, lords and masters, slick up your five wits
For a conundrum match. It looks like nigh all
On us be here.
    [*Calls into the house.*]
     Come, Polly! Come, ye kits!
Dame Puss is in the corner: she'll be catched

That don't peep sharp. Polly, fetch out the bits
O' the gentlemen's visiting-cards.

    [*Looks at the whispering pairs.*]

          I see ye're matched
Already, sirs.

      ALBERTO
   Not I!

      HIKRION
     Nay, I'm thy chum,
Lad.

[*Sylvia and the handmaids come out of the house. Sylvia carries a rustic tray on which lie a violin, a sword, a psalm-book, a paint-brush and a piece of parchment. These she presents before Hikrion with a courtesy. Hikrion holds the things up one after another and appears puzzled.*]

   Ha! These be the cards. I would ye'd scratched
Your initials in 'em, lordings, for I'm mum
If I can read your coats-of-arms. Here, lass,
I'll ask ye just to hand this round to some
O' the gentry-folk, and, masters, when they pass,
Choose your own billets, sith ye were kind enough
To leave 'em.

[*Sylvia passes round the tray; Sandrac, withdrawn from the others, follows her constantly with his eyes.*]

      SYLVIA
  [*Holding the tray before Sob and courtesying.*]
    Yours, sir?

SOB

[*Taking the sword magnificently.*]

Mine's the sword; it has
A savor of my spirit.

SYLVIA

[*To Babblebrook.*]

Yours?

BABBLEBROOK

This volume of
Remorse: "The Book of Psalms."

[*Takes it.*]

SYLVIA

[*Before Pierre.*]

The brush, sir?

PIERRE

[*Taking it.*]

Yes:
With this I imprison mountain peaks.

[*Sylvia passes to Alberto, who seizes his violin eagerly.*]

ALBERTO

Dear love,
I will not leave you any more.

[*Sylvia now hesitates to approach Sandrac, whose eyes regard her piercingly.*]

HIKRION

Well, Miss
Polly?

SYLVIA

Here is a card uncalled for.

HIKRION
                    Nay,
Perhaps his Ravenship —

SANDRAC
[*Steps forward, and, taking the parchment, peers under Sylvia's bonnet.*]
                'Tis mine.
[*He steps back to his side of the scene, while Sylvia retires shyly among the unclaimed handmaids.*]

HIKRION
                        The guess
Comes now, sirs. Hark! As any ass could bray,
I have a daughter, hereamid this lot,
Called Sylvia, as I am pledged to give away,
And she is pledged to bide your choice. She's thought
A handsome prize by many folks, and kings
They've axed her for her hand. But for to be short,
And not to dawdle over loverish things,
This daughter must be found, and they as don't
Guess who she is, must quit their hankerings
And pack off home. But if they guess, this count,
I have a couple of other doubts to speer
At them! So, first, — though 't looks now like ye won't
Take long to pick — choose which ye take for her.
Say: — Who is Sylvia?

BABBLEBROOK, SOB AND PIERRE
[*Kneeling respectively to Fervian, Flurriel and Fresca.*]
                This is she!

HIKRION

             Sir Crow,
What say you?
[*Sandrac extends his hand toward Sylvia, who draws back, shuddering.*]

SANDRAC

This is she.

HIKRION

      How! Think ye, sir,
That Polly Milkmaid — choose again.

SANDRAC

             Not so;
I will abide this choice.

SOB

    Pooh, pooh, he'll take
A serving-maid.

PIERRE

    An artless wench! Pff!

SYLVIA

             Oh,
That I were never born!

HIKRION

[*Scowling.*]
      I cannot break
My word:
    [*To the others.*]
Pack up your hearts!
    [*Points to Sandrac.*]
            He's guessed right.

SANDRAC
[*With triumph.*]
So!
SOB
[*Rising with the others.*]
Odds death! The churning-wench!

PIERRE
Diable!

BABBLEBROOK
Alack!
SANDRAC
[*With a movement toward Sylvia.*]
Lady —

HIKRION
[*Interposing.*]
Hight tight! Sure hit aims slow. Ye can
Answer, mayhap, a second guess. There's three
In all, my hasty master.

SANDRAC
I'm your man
For second and for third.

HIKRION
Hark, then! There be
A treasure of my daughter's. You must tell
Her where it lies; and if ye cannot, ye
Must go your ways.

SYLVIA
Dear spirits, guard me!

SANDRAC
Well:
[*He speaks slowly, never ceasing to look at Sylvia.*]

Sylvia Queen,
Your treasure lies
In the inward eyes
Of the hearts of men.

FELIX
[*Outside.*]
Stand from my path; this time you shall not hold me.

HIKRION
[*To Sylvia.*]
Take heart, my lass.

SYLVIA
I have yet hope, sweet Pater.

HIKRION
[*To Sandrac.*]
Ye have a sharp knack at the guessing. Still
The third guess is the gold key. Maybe later —

SANDRAC
Nay, ask it now!
[*Hikrion hesitates.*]

SYLVIA
Now.

HIKRION
[*Hoarsely.*]
Speak then — right or wrong —
Say: *What is Sylvia?*

SANDRAC
I cannot state a
More magic answer than her own charm'd song:

THE REVERIE

[*He draws the parchment from his gown, opens it and reads: in the first two lines seeming to question Hikrion, toward whom he turns; in the last three lines, addressing Sylvia, and ending with a slight, stately bow, he half reveals, under show of deference to her, the reserved exultation of success.*]

"*Who* is Sylvia? — *What* is she
　　That all her swains commend her?
Holy, fair and wise is she;
　　The heaven such grace did lend her,
That admirèd she might be.

"Is she kind as she is fair?
　　For beauty lives with kindness.

[*Enter Felix; passionate, he is restrained by the cold, majestic form of Somnus.*]

FELIX

Unloose your icy hands! Hind, if you are
A serf of Sylvia's, let me save her now.

[SANDRAC]

"To her eyes love doth repair
　　To help him of his blindness;
And, being helped, inhabits there."

FELIX
[*To Somnus.*]

Off! I will free her. — Sylvia! Love! 'tis I.

SYLVIA
[*To Sandrac.*]

You've won.

HIKRION

My lassie!

[*Turns away and hides his face against Alberto.*]

SANDRAC

[*Taking Sylvia's hand.*]

Till to-night — 'tis long!

Sylvia!

FELIX

[*To Somnus.*]

Let go.

[*Somnus, with imperturbable clutch, still holds him. Felix turns and wrestles with him.*]

My will against your will. We'll match.

[*While Sandrac, in the sunlight of the middle background, kisses the outstretched hand of Sylvia, who turns her face away; while Fervian, Flurriel, Fresca and the suitors on the left, and the six other handmaidens, on the right, gaze at Sandrac in awe and dread, — Felix and Somnus, in the foreground, contrast with these their ghostly figures, wrestling. Felix struggles with an agony of power; Somnus resists with silent, terrible placidity. Presently, while the curtain is slowly descending, Somnus throws Felix, and puts his foot upon him.*]

SOMNUS

Down!

[CURTAIN.]

ACT IV

ACT IV

Scene I:

A cleft in a mountain, at the bend of a torrent. At the back, a steep wall of the mountain, overgrown with stunted cypresses, rises to a jutting cliff of rock, which overtops the bed of the stream; above this the sky. The stream itself emerges precipitately from a cavern on the left, whence, in a deep, rock-strewn gulley, it rushes out, first straight, and then — at the back of scene — bending to the right and downward, disappears behind the steep back wall aforesaid. At the right front, a mountain path — visible for some distance — enters the scene and leads, by its right fork, to the rough foreground, which forms the front bank of the stream and the larger part of the stage; by its left fork, turning downward into the rocky bed of the stream. At left, near the front, a gigantic, lightning-withered oak tosses its sere limbs upward and outward over the torrent, near its egress from the cavern. All these scenic features, however, are but dimly or transiently discernable, for dusk masses of mist roll through the scene and down the torrent, shifting, closing and disparting at the whim of intermittent and passionate gusts of wind.

As the scene opens, enter, right, along the pass, Felix.

FELIX

What rush of streams precipitant
Makes in my ears mill-noises? Why

Must I outface this blinding gale
Of mountain surf? — Still none to answer!
Come, then, I'll find an airy alcove,
And pedestal myself in patience
Here on the stair of this gusty castle
Of fog, till Sylvia comes, to guide
Me up and on.

[*He gropes his way to a log, green with moss, which has fallen across the stream. On the front end of this he sits. Here he is suddenly roused from his reverie by a wild gust and a voice, seeming to come from the branches of the tree.*]

A VOICE

Felix!

FELIX

Who speaks?

THE VOICE

She will not come; thou art alone.

FELIX

Whom speak you of?

THE VOICE

Of Sylvia.

FELIX

                            She
Will come.

THE VOICE
A merry trysting-place!
[The wind howls in the ravine and through the branches of the oak.]

FELIX
[Rising.]
Strange!   Such incorporal discourse
As this is elvish: more elusive
Even than my own.
[Peers up, from beneath the tree.]
    Is there a creature
In the branches?   I can see but faintly
For fog. — I must have fancied it.
And yet I know the voice of fancy
Is often the just premonitor
Of truth.,   Not, though, when it is phantasm,
Faint, blurr'd and undefined like this,
Without distinguishable image
For reason to seize on.   For fancy
Is pied and vivid; this is phantasm.

A SECOND VOICE
Felix!

FELIX
What now? — another voice?

SECOND VOICE
Go back; return to Arden.

FELIX

No;

She bade me to await her here.

SECOND VOICE

But why?

FELIX

For nothing ill, that's sure.

SECOND VOICE

Is not this an ill pass?

FELIX

Not if

She come.

SECOND VOICE

But where is she?

FELIX

She comes.

FIRST AND SECOND VOICES

Where?

FELIX

In my heart's assurance.

SECOND VOICE

Ho.

His heart's assurance!

[*A wild cataract of laughter leaps from the boughs and dies away down the ravine. Felix peers again into the tree.*]

FELIX

Stranger still!

Are those eyes there that, like two embers,

Pry at me through this smoke of mist?
I'll test it with this oak-gall.

[*Felix picks up a gall and throws it into the tree. A dim cat-like form bounds from a branch and disappears in the fog.*]

                       Ah!
This voice has limbs — it leaps — a lynx!

[*Pursuing it, he lifts a rock, which he hurls after it down the ravine.*]

Now caterwaul! — The flood shall drown
Your pitch.
         [*Returning slowly.*]
           In this gray land of cypress,
The elements and dumb creatures
Wag tongues in mockery of men.

[*A loud uproar of applause and hand-clapping bursts from the branches.*]

          A THIRD VOICE
Felix!
             FELIX
    Once more? — What ogre-oak
Is this, which has a hundred heads?

           THIRD VOICE
A hundred heads!
     [*A reëcho of applause and of clappings.*]
              We are tongue-waggers;
We will not wag of you — not you!
We will not clap for you — not you!

We will not cry your name — nay, nay!
From you forever we fly away.

[*The sun breaks for an instant through the fog, as a silvery flock of pigeons fly from amid the dead branches and, with a great flutter of wings, vanish in the mist of the ravine. Felix watches them as they disappear.*]

FELIX
Your wings are beautiful, and yet
Your voices sound as hoarse as ravens'
Now in my ears, that are inured
To Sylvia's soft chidings, more
Precious to me than all your praises.

[*He has hardly ceased, when there resounds a chorus of piercing hisses; while from the chasm, where the pigeons disappeared, a flock of crows, winging through the obscure air, settles hissing upon the branches of the oak, which again is involved in mist.*]

THE FIRST VOICE
Felix!

FELIX
What! Are you back again?

SECOND VOICE
We're come again to change our tune:
To sing to you like this, this, this!
We'll leave no more — we're come to stay;
We'll stick by you for ay and — ay.

[*Hisses again.*]

FELIX

Why, now your feathers fit your throats.
I thank you for your chorus; it
Is helpful to my purposes.
For virtues are invulnerable;
And as for my shortcomings, if
You'll hiss them only half as harsh
As I do, you and I together
Shall put them soon to shame; and so
I thank you for your comradeship.

THIRD VOICE

Why, then we will not stay.

THE OTHER VOICES
Nay! Nay!

[*The crows fly away again down the ravine, hissing fainter and fainter.*]

FELIX

Now what a twinge would vice my sides
To crow with laughter, at the rout
Of such hypocrisy, had I
Not read long since — writ large in tears
Of gay philosophers — this warning
To fools: "Laugh, fool; but laugh not *at*."

[*Starting, he peers down the mountain pass.*]

Ah! see: the "silvery dove" returns.
Sylvia!

[*Enter Sylvia, as a spirit.*]

SYLVIA

You have waited long,
And I came not.

FELIX

I could have waited
My latest breath, so to have carried
This vision of you with me to darkness.
O Sylvia!

SYLVIA

To save us both
I am come here to guide you. Do
You know this stream?

FELIX

I do not know,
Nor where I am, but that I walk
With you.

SYLVIA

This is a shoulder of
That fabled mount Parnassus, which
At the world's dawning flung afar
Its shadow over men. — This torrent
Springs from its heart of olden marble
Deep-hid in the dim labyrinths
Of yonder cavern, whence it pours
Here headlong; farther, at that bend,
It plunges downward, ever discoursing
In its own throat, till at the base
It feeds the stagnant marsh of Lethe.

FELIX
So this is Lethe stream?

SYLVIA
     'Tis near
The bright head waters of that stream,
Whose springing fountain has a virtue
Which lower it loses in the marsh;
For where it bubbles up, its waters
May be transported without losing
Their tincture of oblivion.
But they who seek forgetfulness
From Lethe marsh, go browsing there
Gregarious, like herded cattle
To pasture, and when they have drunk,
They rot into the swamp like stumps.

FELIX
But what of them who drink its source
Transported from the secret spring
In yonder cavern?

SYLVIA
    They are dealt
Instant annihilation, like
Eagles midair, whom the fiery blade
Of lightning severs. For Felix, know,
Oblivion of evil may
Be compassed in either of two ways:—
By Time, a fat, relapsing sluggard,
That sits with Death on the bog of Lethe,

Oft at whose summons Oblivion lags
To take part in our funerals;
Or else, by man's own Will, in his
Self-mastered fortress, on the heights
Of this same mountain: there, his will,
By a mandate instantaneous
Hurls down the giddied evil in
The shadow of forgetfulness,
Where, falling, it dies apoplex'd
By its own impotence.

FELIX

                Oh, then,
Guide me to clamber to that source
Where I may fill my spirit's flask
To bear to Sandrac and to all
My creatures that constrain you. Fain
Would I forget them with my will,
And drug them with a glittering draught
From Lethe's supreme fount.

SYLVIA

                So only,
Our love may be redeemed; for soon
At sundown, Sandrac I must wed,
Unless, by then, from your own hand,
He drinks the obliterating drug.

FELIX

He shall! — Is this the path? Oh, come!
I wait like powder to be flashed.
The torrent beckons me. — Your hand!

[*He starts to cross the torrent on the log.*]

SYLVIA

Wait! — Hearts can never clamber there
Unshrived.

FELIX

What shame still have not I
Confessed?

SYLVIA

But now, as I came here,
A wounded lynx sprang in my path
And, fawning helpless, died there.

FELIX

Him
I killed, for on this bough he sat
And laughed a hellish laugh at me.

SYLVIA

And you would kill a foolish creature
For your own ignorance?

FELIX

Not so;
It gibed my sins.

SYLVIA

How could it gibe,
Your sins — and not your ignorance?

FELIX

[*Moved.*]
I hate my thought and act.

SYLVIA
[*Gently.*]
My friend

FELIX
And yet it spoke, and so did flocks
Of birds that perched in these same boughs.

SYLVIA
It was not they who spoke. You heard
The inmates of this oak; the trunk
Is hollow, and within it dwell
The three mist-mothers. It is they
Who ravel the Norns' weavings. See,
Here in the tree bole is a door. —
I'll knock, for we have business here.
  [*Sylvia knocks; voices answer from within.*]

FIRST VOICE
Who raps?

SECOND VOICE
'Tis the woodpecker.

THIRD VOICE
Shut her out — shut her out! She hunts for worms.

FELIX
These voices are the same I heard.

THE THREE VOICES
[*Singing within the oak.*]

Lithe and nimble, blithe and nimble,
Spinner's loom, and stitcher's thimble,
 Ply the thread for time's untwisting.
Block the shuttle! Break the spindle!
Dream shall wane and deed shall dwindle,
 Where the mist-mothers hold their trysting.
  What Norna knit
  Pluck, bit by bit!
 Piecemeal, tatter and scatter it!

 All of triumph — all of travail,
  Ravel, mother, ravel!

FELIX
What song is this?

SYLVIA
'Tis one they sing
At work, as they wind the grand designs
And intricate thought of patient years
Back on their ball of primal mist.
I'll knock again more loud.
[*She knocks again.*]

THE FIRST VOICE
[*Within.*]
   Who raps?

SYLVIA
Sylvia!

FIRST VOICE
'Tis the dove!

SECOND VOICE

She hunts for seeds.

THIRD VOICE

Fetch her in! Fetch her in!

[*The door in the bark opens, and forth leap three female figures, whose wraith-like garments, mingling with the mists, sway on the winds, and vaguely define the forms of an old, white-haired woman, a matron in the prime of life, and a light-footed damsel. They greet Sylvia and courtesy round and round her.*]

THE WHITE-HAIRED

Welcome, white dove! Welcome to Letheland.

THE THREE

Welcome! Welcome!

THE WHITE-HAIRED

[*Stops suddenly, points at Felix and addresses the Matron.*]
Mother, who is it?

THE MATRON

[*Doing the same and addressing the Damsel.*]
Mother, what is it?

THE DAMSEL

[*Addressing the White-Haired and running away.*]
Mother, 'tis a man!

THE THREE

[*Rush into the tree, closing the bark again.*]
A man!

FELIX
Are these the wives of Somnus?

SYLVIA
                    Yes.
FELIX
But why did each say "mother" to
Her neighbor?

SYLVIA
            'Tis because, from damsel
To granny, they are their own offspring.
For they are barren to create
New fruitful forms, to populate
The nebulous ether; yet they are
Wondrous prolific of themselves.
Thus, ever when these fogs grow big
With lusty winds, even as a bubble
Distends and, coalescing with
Its in-blown substance, bursts to beget
Its twin — so each gives birth to the other,
With most unprofitable anguish
Tormenting their void wombs.

FELIX
                    How strange!
An infinite monotony
Of metamorphosis!

SYLVIA
[Raps again.]
Open, mother!

THE FIRST VOICE

Nay, nay!

SECOND VOICE

A man!

THIRD VOICE

He'll rob us of our ravellings!

SYLVIA

Nay, he is bodiless, save as
We too are bodied. Have no fear,
But fetch me forth the woof of a snarl
Was woven by a youth called Felix
And named " A Garland to Sylvia."

FIRST VOICE

Is he without there harmless?

SECOND VOICE

Ay, is he harmless?

THIRD VOICE

Who'll be his voucher?

SYLVIA

Harmless he is. Fear not. — Come forth.

[*They come forth again, more timidly, bringing a crooked piece of tapestry, woven loosely of silver, gray, green and gold threads, depicting a wood, with grouped figures among the trees. The whole, save for one form in a black gown, dull and opaque, glisters with a phosphorescent light, which makes the figures appear to move, enter and depart, so as incessantly to form new scenes and groupings.*]

THE WHITE-HAIRED
Greeting, white dove! greeting from Letheland!
THE THREE
[*Courtesying.*]
Greeting!
SYLVIA
[*Taking the tapestry from the Three, she hands it to Felix.*]
Look there!
FELIX
[*Fascinated.*]
My play!
THE THREE
Nay, nay, nay, 'tis ours!
[*Snatching it from Felix, they guard it jealously.*]
SYLVIA
Peace!   Give it me.
THE WHITE-HAIRED
Not I, he will steal it.
THE OTHER TWO
Not we, he will steal it.
SYLVIA
Why, keep it then, and hold it, while
I take the end of the ravelling thread.
THE WHITE-HAIRED
Mother, didst hear?

THE MATRON

Mother, she'll ravel it.

THE DAMSEL

Mother, we'll make merry.

THE THREE

[*Laughing, reach to Sylvia a fine luminous thread.*]
Here it is.   Here it is!
[*Sylvia takes it and starts toward the log.*]

FELIX

[*Interposing.*]

What will you do?   Destroy it?

SYLVIA

Nay,
You must do that.   I can but lead
If you consent.   Hold here the thread
With me, and I will guide you, by
Its slender light, to Lethe's source.
Now! — Do you will it?
[*Felix, hesitating, gazes on the fabric of his play, which one of the mist-women holds, while the other two, with dexterous fingerings, prepare to unravel it.*]

FELIX

Oh, how fair
A tapestry I dreamed of weaving,
When first I started fancy's shuttle:
So fair, that, in its golden lights

And green, the marvelling eyes of men
Should own that heaven and earth were blended;
That in this web of sylvan half-light
Nature and man had found a symbol
Of their essential truth of beauty.

SYLVIA

But was it so?

FELIX

No, for a shadow
Inwove its night in my brightest noon-day:
A phantasm, cast by my self-love,
That barred my vision, and marred the clear
And fair design.

SYLVIA

Then why do you
Stand dubious, my Felix?

FELIX

Oh,
It is not doubt, but bitter love,
Heart-yearning for a strange miscarriage,
Which, had it come to birth, perchance
Had awed the world with beauty. Ah!
But this no more! for out of failure
Comes faith. Now to the great solution!
Ravel out, you mothers of the mist!
This fabric of my buzzing brain
Whirl into filaments as fine
As gossamer, and let the winds

Dissolve them. I myself will pull
The ravelling thread. — Now, Sylvia, lead!

SYLVIA

Hold fast the thread, and here the flask
To fill at Lethe's fountain. Follow!

FELIX

Before me, you: Behind — the play!

[*Crossing the log, they skirt the torrent by a narrow ridge-path on its left bank, and, ascending into the dim cavern, lighted only by the luminous guiding-thread, are visible as far as an abrupt bend, where they disappear. From within the cavern, however, their voices are still heard above the torrent — ever more faintly.*]

Sylvia!
                  SYLVIA
    Felix!
                  FELIX
       Sylvia!

SYLVIA

Higher!

[*Meantime, in the foreground, beneath the oak, the dwindling play-tapestry, held by the White-Haired, is being ravelled by the two other mist-wives. These, with whirling arms, whip away the thread in luminous skeins; in doing so, their swaying limbs keep time to the cadence of their song, till, at its close, as the tapestry wholly disappears, a great gust of fog envelops them in the act of returning to the hollow oak.*]

THE THREE MOTHERS

Out of smother and darkness, mother,
Tell us, who shall shape another
    Woof like the one that we're unweaving?
Many and many a nobler weaver
Shall toil anew, but none can ever
    Recapture the soul's conceiving.
        Whirl a skein
        Of joy and pain —
    Then wind it on the world again!

    All of triumph, all of travail
        Ravel, mother, ravel!

See this tangle, wrought in wrangle,
Like an ill-hung chime a-jangle —
    Better its fabric fell to ground!
Better or worse, worse or better,
The misty fingers brook no fetter,
    And leave not a thread, not a sound.
        Thought in its rune,
        Love at its noon,
    Like beauty's bubble, is burst — is gone!

[*Just as they disappear in the oak, a flood of sunlight slants through the upper mists, revealing above the obscured torrent, the jutting bluff of the mountain, and above that a rift of the blue sky. Against this rift, Sylvia and Felix, emerging from underground, come forward upon the bluff.*]

FELIX

The sunlight!

SYLVIA

Is the flask filled full?

FELIX

Behold it glittering to the brim
With bright oblivion.

SYLVIA

Brave heart!
So shall you bring it back to Arden.
There, when your creatures all have drunk,
Behold what shall result — look down!

[*Sylvia points from the bluff to where, in the bed of the torrent, a varied group of figures have emerged from the mountain-pass, and are being driven down the rocky stream by Somnus. The first two are the forms of Babblebrook and Sob, disputing dumbly; then follows Pierre, with easel under his arm, talking to himself; behind him, Sandrac, with his proud smile and pace of meditation.*]

FELIX

What is the portent of this pageant?

SYLVIA

A vision and a prophecy
Of what shall come to pass, when you
Shall keep your vow to me.

FELIX

        All, all,
To Lethe?

SYLVIA
Do you weep?

FELIX
In thanks
And joy, that they shall menace you
No more.

SYLVIA
Then is there none you would
Reclaim? Look down.

FELIX
Even him?

[*Behind Somnus, and apart from the other descending figures, passes downward the lithe figure of Alberto. Stepping from rock to rock with unconscious agility, he seems to pour his soul forth to the ravine through his violin. Yet no sound is heard from the swaying instrument, and Alberto, with the others, disappears at the downward bend of the stream.*

From the verge of the cliff Felix makes an imploring gesture.]

Alberto!

[CURTAIN.]

ACT IV: Scene II

An opening in the wood near Hikrion's cottage. A rough semicircle of trees festooned with ropes of flowers, interwoven with blossoming vines, forms as it were a solid garland for the scene. Through this are only two narrow openings: one on the left, overlapt by the circlet in the fore ground, is not visible; through the other, on the right, the last horizontal rays of the sun illumine the flowery background. In the centre of the scene is raised a double, rustic throne. Standing beside this is discovered Hikrion, clad in a robe and cowl of golden green.

HIKRION

First, I must do the priestly offices
For this upstart, who prigs away my lass —
My darlingest Sylvia; then, may I please!
The other three, seeing the sorry pass
They've brought their mistress to — Fervian and Flurry
And Fresca with 'em — they've sworn also, as
A kind o' penance-game to cheer the worry,
To wed these wooing crittern — Sob and Pierre
And Babblebrook, rather'n see Sylvia sorry
Alone. And me this crow-groom Sandrac there —
Me being a kind o' parson to the peasant
Folks, swapping lies and preaching 'em to pair —
Says to me: "Papa Hikrion, come, be pleasant
And be our priest; a woodland service makes
Two one, as well as Westminster." So I,
For Sylvia's sake, agree on't, though it breaks
The pipe o' mirth within me. But now's nigh
Their time of coming.—'Tis a bonny scene,

Though I be praiser of the work that's mine:
I've tidied out a chapel here in the green
And hollowed wood-cups for the wedding-wine. —
Hark: now they come.

      [*Alberto's violin is heard outside.*]

                The boy plays sad as a pine
When winter's coming in.

[*Enter, left, the wedding procession, walking slowly to the accompaniment of Alberto's violin, which renders a minor variation of the melody "Who is Sylvia?" Enter first — two by two — six Handmaids, carrying each a garland of flowers. With these they form an arbor, the garlands being held aloft and touching, to form the arch. Beneath this, in pairs, pass, in sequence, Sob and Flurriel, Babblebrook and Fervian, Pierre and Fresca. The couples, as they issue forth, join garlands to form an extension of the bower, so that Sandrac and Sylvia — the former still dressed in his black gown, the latter as a bride — enter the scene through a living bower of maidens, suitors and flowers, and pass to where Hikrion awaits them, in front of the double throne. Here Sandrac takes his stand by the right throne, Sylvia by the left, while the others break the bower and group themselves on either side. After Sandrac and Sylvia, Alberto enters alone. Last of all, enter Felix and Somnus, who do not pass through the bower. As Alberto ceases to play, Sandrac speaks.*]

SANDRAC

Now, Sylvia, Apollo plays my Cupid
And shoots you with his dying shaft of gold;
And now, ere these fresh day-flowers here be droopèd,
And you and your bright bevy change your mould

To moonlit spirits, we will wed. What you bid
Shall be my law. I wish you joys star-fold.

SYLVIA

Wishes unwilled are like unplanted seeds:
They dry in the brain, like wheat-ears in a barn,
That, kept too long, lose power to get their breeds.

SANDRAC

What have I left unsown, that I should earn
Such sad reproof?
SYLVIA
    Live wishes sprout in deeds; —
But shall we to the service?

SANDRAC
     That we will.
But first, that all may hail the joy that's mine
Let every bridegroom here his beaker fill
And drink "A Health to Sylvia!" Come, wine, wine,
Good Pater Hikrion.

HIKRION

[*Muttering, as he pours out wine from a leathern vat.*]
    By Selenus, I'll
Not be dubbed *Pater* by that beak o' thine.

[*While Hikrion pours the wine, into five wooden cups, Felix
 reaches over his shoulder, and pours into each cup liquid
 from his own flask.*]

FELIX

Drop, Lethe, drop! Your bane emancipates
My love, and makes this murder innocent.

THE REVERIE

[HIKRION]

[*Passing a cup to Sandrac.*]

Here, Master Groom, ye'll find this a true rill
From Pan's own vineyard.

FELIX

Yes, Sandrac, you will find it heady. Try it.

SANDRAC

[*Taking the cup.*]

      So? Pass round, then, pass
Still round, old fellow.
[*Hikrion passes cups to Sob, Babblebrook and Pierre; lastly to Alberto.*]

HIKRION

Drink too, lad!

ALBERTO

      No, no,
I am not thirsty.

HIKRION

    Pho! this here's prime class;
'Twill make the music mount in thee. Come!

ALBERTO

[*Taking the cup.*]

        Oh,
Well!

FELIX

Could he not spare that one! Alberto mine!

SANDRAC

 Drink! A health to Sylvia! Now, each cup
On high! Long life to Sylvia! Sylvia ho!

THE SUITORS
Long life to Sylvia!

SANDRAC
[*Pointing to the west.*]

See! My star is up,
And the world's day-god sets. Drink this with me,
Sylvia!

[*He extends the cup to her. Instantly Felix steps forward and
empties his flask into it.*]

FELIX
The dregs — here, have it all!
[*Flinging his flask away.*]
So, Sandrac, drink:
Drink deep as your own joy — and Lethe.

SANDRAC
[*As Sylvia draws back.*]

Still you hesitate to sup?
Then first will I: and then — your lips!

[*He drinks. Simultaneously, as the other Suitors drink
also, the twilight deepens into blackness. Out of the dark
sounds the voice of Somnus.*]

SOMNUS
Felix,
Farewell!

THE VOICE OF FELIX
Farewell, Somnus!

[*Swiftly, a dawning moonlight illumines the garland, and
reveals Felix, clad in his black gown of the Prologue,
standing where Sandrac had stood beside Sylvia. To-*

gether they mount the rustic throne. Sandrac and the Suitors have disappeared. Hikrion's green robe and cowl have altered to a garb of hides and wreath of grape leaves, clothing a shrewd-eyed Satyr. With lifted pipe, he leads an entering throng of sylvan Spirits. These, encircling in their dance the double throne, shower garlands at the feet of Felix and Sylvia.]

THE SPIRITS

Then to Sylvia let us sing
   That Sylvia is excelling!
She excels each mortal thing
   Upon the dull earth dwelling;
To her garlands let us bring!

[CURTAIN.]

FINIS